THE BIBLE OF LATIN AMERICAN CUISINE

10 Countries, 50 recipes cookbook for beginners to start making delicious plates with traditional Latin flavor

By
Paola Siciliano

Contents

Pabellon Criollo

Pabellon criollo is a traditional recipe in Venezuela. Black beans and rice are accompanied by tender slices of flank steak that have been cooked with tomatoes.

 Serving: 6   **Time: 2 hr 45 minutes**

INGREDIENTS

- 1½ lb flank steak
- 2 tsp bouillon cubes
- 4 clove cloves minced garlic
- 6 tbsp vegetable oil
- 1½ tsp salt
- 1 cup white rice, soaked in water
- 1 cup chopped onions
- 1 15-oz can black beans
- 1 tsp chicken bouillon cube
- 1½ tsp cumin
- ½ tsp garlic powder
- 1 tbsp vinegar
- 2 tbsp butter
- 2 medium tomatoes, diced

INSTRUCTIONS

1. In a pot, add the flank steak and bouillon, and cover with water. Bring to a boil and simmer for 1½ hours or until is tender. Remove from heat and set aside.
2. In a pot, heat 4tbsp oil and cook half of the garlic for 1 to 2 minutes.
3. Add 2 cups water and 1 tsp salt and bring to a boil. Then add the rice, cover with lid and simmer for 10-15 minutes. Turn off the heat and leave the rice covered for 5 minutes more.
4. In a skillet, heat 2 tbsp vegetable oil and sauté half of the onions with the remaining garlic until softened.
5. Stir in the can of black beans, ½ cup water, chicken bouillon, cumin, garlic powder, vinegar, and ½ tsp salt. Simmer over low heat for 10 minutes or until the liquid evaporated.
6. Slice the cooked steak and shred the larger pieces into bite-size pieces with your hands.
7. In a skillet, heat 2 tbsp butter and sauté the remaining onions until softened. Stir in the tomatoes, 1 cup of the steak pan juices, and the sliced steak. Simmer for 3-5 minutes. Remove from heat and cool.
8. On a serving plate, place the meat, tomatoes, beans and rice. Serve with fried plantains on the side and enjoy!

Tequeños

Tequeños are an easy recipe and so delicious! Tequeños sticks of white cheese wrapped with sweet dough (homemade) and then fried to golden perfection. One won't be enough!.

 Serving: 14   **Time: 1 hr 15 minutes**

INGREDIENTS

- 2 cups all-purpose flour
- 1 tsp Kosher salt
- 6 tbsp cold butter, ¼-inch cubes
- 1 large egg, lightly beaten
- 6 tbsp cold water
- 12 oz queso blanco (½ x ½ x 2½ inch slices)
- Peanut oil, for frying

INSTRUCTIONS

1. In a bowl of food processor, add salt and flour and pulse to mix. Add butter evenly over flour and pulse until butter is cut into pea-size pieces. Then transfer dough to a large bowl.
2. Add in egg and water. Press the mixture down against side of bowl until it forms into a ball.
3. Press dough into a disc, wrap tightly in plastic wrap and place in fridge for 30 minutes.
4. Unwrap dough and place on a lightly floured surface. Roll out into a square 1/8-inch thick. Cut off edges to create a 12-inch square. Cut the square into strips ¾-inch wide.
5. Take one strip of dough and drape end over top of one cheese slice. Wrap entire cheese slice in dough on a diagonal, overlapping dough. Cover bottom of cheese slice in dough and pinch edges close to fully seal.
6. Repeat with remaining cheese slices.
7. Add oil to a cast iron skillet (fill ¾-inch of oil). Heat oil to 400°F over high heat. Add tequeños and cook until brown for 3-5 minutes.
8. Line a plate with paper towel and transfer tequeños to it. Allow to cool for 1-2 minutes, then serve immediately.

Arepa Reina Pepiada

Arepas were being cooked by Venezuela in South America. This is so delicious recipe to serve as a side dish. You will fall in love with these easy and versatile South American cornbread rounds!

 Serving: 6   **Time: 1 hr 20 minutes**

INGREDIENTS

- 2 cups warm water
- 1 tbsp oil
- 1 tsp salt
- 2 cups masa arepa

Filling:

- 1 lb chicken breast boneless
- 6 cups of chicken broth
- 1½ avocado cut into cubes
- ¾ onion chopped
- 1½ garlic clove
- 6 tbsp mayonnaise
- ¾ cup of peas
- Salt, to taste

INSTRUCTIONS

1. In a bowl, mix the water, oil and salt. Stir in masa arepa and cover the bowl with a tea towel. Set aside for 10 minutes.
2. Add 1 tbsp water if the dough seems too dry.
3. Preheat your oven to 350° F.
4. Divide the dough into 6 pieces. Shape them like a disc.
5. Brush the arepas with oil for 5 minutes.
6. Bake for 20 minutes. Let cool, slice and serve.
7. Meanwhile, cook the chicken breast, previously seasoned with salt and pepper, inside the chicken broth on medium heat for 15 minutes. Then shred the chicken.
8. In a pan, heat oil and sauté the onion and garlic for 2 minutes. Add the shredded chicken and stir for 5 minutes.
9. Combine the avocado, green peas, chicken and mayo in a bowl. Mix well and add a pinch of salt and pepper.
10. Fill the arepa with chicken mixture and serve!

Bollo Pelón

This is a family-style, authentic and delicious dish from Venezuela. Bollo pelón is comprised of meat-balls wrapped in arepa dough, combining amazing flavors for a comfort meal.

Serving: 14   Time: 55 minutes

INGREDIENTS

- 2 tbsp corn oil
- 1 cup onion, chopped
- 3 clove garlic, minced
- ½ cup green bell pepper, diced
- ½ cup leeks, sliced
- ¼ cup scallions, sliced
- 1 lb ground beef
- Salt and pepper, to taste
- 2 tbsp tomato paste
- 4 tbsp sweet red wine
- 23-25 green olives stuffed with red pepper, sliced
- 3 tbsp of capers, drained

Sauce:
- 2 tbsp corn oil
- 2 cups onion, chopped
- 1 (28 oz) can diced tomatoes
- Salt and pepper, to taste

Dough:
- 2½ cups of chicken broth, warm
- 3 cups harina pan
- 2 tbsp of corn oil
- 8 oz of queso fresco, crumbled

INSTRUCTIONS

Filling:
1. In a saucepan, heat the oil and sauté the onion until translucent.
2. Stir in the garlic, pepper, leeks, and scallions. Cook for 5 minutes.
3. Stir in ground beef. Break the meat with a wooden spoon and season with salt and pepper to taste. Cook for 5 minutes or until brown.
4. Stir in the tomato paste, wine, olives, and capers. Simmer for 10-15 minutes, or until liquid has evaporated. Remove from heat.

Sauce:
5. In a saucepan, heat the corn oil. Sauté the onion for 3 minutes or until transparent.
6. Stir in the diced tomatoes and season with salt and pepper to taste.
7. Cover and simmer for 20-25 minutes. Remove from heat and set aside.

Dough:
8. Mix chicken broth and Harina pan until has no lumps. Let stand for 5 minutes then add the corn oil and knead until smooth. Divide the dough into 14 equal-sized balls. Set aside.

Assemble:
9. Take a ball of dough and make a hole in the center with your finger, big enough to place the filling. Add 1-2 tsp of the filling. Close bringing the edges together carefully with your fingers. Re-form into a ball again. Repeat until all the dough is finished.

Patacón Zuliano

This is a very common Latin recipe of Venezuelan. You can serve this sandwich as a side dish. Very common in food stalls and restaurants! It is also called Venezuelan Patacón.

 Serving: 4   **Time: 30 minutes**

INGREDIENTS

- ¼ cup canola oil
- 1 unripe plantain, peeled and halved crosswise
- ¼ cup mayonnaise
- 2 sprigs cilantro
- ½ avocado, pitted and peeled
- Kosher salt, to taste
- Ground black pepper, to taste
- 1 cup shredded roast beef
- 2 leaves green-leaf lettuce
- 2 slices tomato

INSTRUCTIONS

1. In a skillet, heat oil over medium-high. Cook plantain halves for 3 minutes or until light brown, flipping once.
2. Place the cooked plantain on a cutting board and divide each in half lengthwise, keeping them hinged on the curved side.
3. Cut sides down and flatten each into a ¼-inch thick round disk by using a plate.
4. Fry the flattened plantains again until crisp for 4 minutes. Then transfer to paper towels to drain.
5. In a blender, add the mayonnaise, cilantro, avocado and puree until smooth. Season with salt and pepper. Then add to a bowl.
6. In a bowl, add the avocado puree and beef. Toss to coat well.
7. Place beef mixture on one plantain disk and top with lettuce and tomato. Cover with another disk.

Asado

Asado is a delicious dish introduced by Argentina. It's a complete food to eat for a time. It can be shared as a lunch or dinner.

 Serving: 3   **Time: 1 hour**

INGREDIENTS

- 1½ lbs pork
- 1 tsp allspice powder
- ½ cup soy sauce
- 1/3 cup brown sugar
- 1 tsp garlic minced
- 2 tbsp cooking rice wine
- ¼ tsp salt
- 2 cups water

INSTRUCTIONS

1. In a bowl, mix the soy sauce, spice powder, garlic, cooking rice wine, and salt.
2. Add pork and toss to coat well. Marinade for 1 hour.
3. Heat a pot. Add pork along with the marinade and water. Bring to boil.
4. Stir in brown sugar and simmer for 40 minutes, flip the meat at halftime.
5. Allow cooling for about 10 minutes then slice the meat.
6. Transfer to a serving plate and top with the thick sauce then serve.

Chimichurri

Chimichurri is the best accompaniment to any barbecued meats in Argentina. You can serve it as a dressing on salads!

 Serving: 8   **Time: 10 minutes**

INGREDIENTS

- ½ cup olive oil
- 2 tbsp red wine vinegar
- ½ cup finely chopped parsley
- 3-4 cloves garlic, minced
- 1 tbsp chopped red chilies, deseeded
- ¾ tsp dried oregano
- 1 level tsp coarse salt
- ½ tsp pepper, to taste

INSTRUCTIONS

1. Prepare all the ingredients.
2. In a bowl, add all the ingredients and mix well.
3. Set aside to rest for 2 hours to release all of the flavors.
4. You can refrigerate for 24 hours if needed.
5. Serve.

Alfajores

A delicious combination of crumbly sugar cookies sandwiched together with dulce de leche. Alfajores is so delicious recipe to serve as a dessert.

Serving: 16   **Time: 30 minutes**

INGREDIENTS

- 4 oz unsalted butter or 1 stick
- ¼ cup sugar
- 1 egg yolk
- 1 tsp vanilla extract
- ½ cup + 2tbsp all-purpose flour
- ½ cup + 2tbsp cornstarch corn-flour
- 5 tbsp dulce de leche

INSTRUCTIONS

1. In a food processor, add butter and sugar. Pulse until creamy.
2. Add the egg yolk and vanilla. Blend to mix. Add the flour and cornstarch. Mix and form a ball. Wrap and refrigerate for 30 minutes.
3. Preheat the oven to 350° F. Line a baking sheet. Repeat with the rest of the dough.
4. Bake the cookies for about 10 minutes until just light brown and should be very pale. Allow cooling on the wire rack.
5. Add a small spoonful of dulce de leche to half cookies and press another half on top softly.
6. Roll the outside in coconut or sugar, optional.

Argentinian Empanadas

There are as many variations of empanadas as there are cooks in Argentina. These Empanadas are filled with ground beef meat. The Argentine empanada is small, just two or three delicious bites.

 Serving: 6   Time: 1 hr 45 minutes

INGREDIENTS

- 3 tbsp olive oil, divided
- 2 lb ground beef
- 2 medium onions, chopped
- 2 small red bell peppers, chopped
- Kosher salt, freshly ground pepper
- 3 tbsp ground cumin
- 2 tbsp sweet paprika
- 1 tbsp dried oregano
- ¼ tsp cayenne pepper
- 1½ cups chicken stock or broth
- 2 tsp sugar
- ½ cup raisins
- 3 (12) packages puff pastry dough
- ½ cup pitted green olives, rinsed, cut in half

INSTRUCTIONS

1. In a pot, heat 2 tbsp oil and add beef. Cook and break up with a spoon, until browned for 6-8 minutes. Transfer the beef to a bowl and leave fats in pan.
2. Add onion, bell peppers, and remaining 1 tbsp oil to pan. Sauté until tender for 6–8 minutes. Season with salt and black pepper.
3. Stir in cumin, paprika, oregano, and cayenne. Cook for a minute.
4. Stir in chicken stock, cooked beef, sugar, 4 tsp salt, and ¼ tsp black pepper.
5. Bring to a boil and simmer for 15–20 minutes or liquid is evaporated. Stir in raisins. Transfer to bowl, allow to cool, cover, and refrigerate for 3 hours.
6. Preheat the oven to 375°F. Line a baking tray with parchment paper.
7. Place the 6 dough on work surface. Top with 2 tbsp filling and 2 olive halves. Brush with water on the edges. Fold round over filling and pinch edges to seal. Crimp the edges with fork and place on baking tray.
8. Bake for 25-35 minutes or until golden brown, rotating tray halfway through.

Carbonada

Carbonada is a delicious stew, and wonderful for when the weather turns chilly. You can serve it with cornbread and a green salad.

Serving: 8   Time: 2 hours

INGREDIENTS

- 1/3 cup olive oil
- 1 large onion, chopped
- 1 green pepper, chopped
- 2 cloves garlic, minced
- 1½ lb beef, 1-inch pieces
- 1 (14.5-oz) can stewed tomatoes
- 2 cups beef broth
- 3 sweet potatoes, cubed
- 2 white potatoes, cubed
- 2 tbsp sugar
- 1 large winter squash, cubed
- 1 cup (7 oz) dried apricots, roughly chopped
- Kosher salt, to taste
- Freshly ground black pepper, to taste
- 1 cup frozen corn

INSTRUCTIONS

1. Heat oil in a pot. Add the onions, green pepper, and garlic until golden and soft. Sauté for about 10 minutes.
2. Stir in the beef and cook on medium-high heat, turning to brown all sides.
3. Stir in the stewed tomatoes, beef broth, sweet potatoes, white potatoes, sugar, squash, and apricots. Bring to boil
4. Lower the heat, cover and simmer over low heat for 1 hour.
5. Season with salt and pepper to taste. Adjust thickness with beef broth. Cook for about 30 minutes longer, until beef is tender.
6. Add the frozen corn, and simmer for 5 to 10 minutes. Serve.

Feijoada

Brazilian Feijoada is pork and black bean. You can serve it with farofa, toasted cassava flour. Soak the beans overnight before cooking the stew.

 Serving: 10   **Time: 2 hr 45 minutes**

INGREDIENTS

- 1 lb dry black beans, soaked
- 1 tbsp olive oil
- 4 oz slab bacon (rind removed), diced
- 1 lb pork ribs, individual ribs
- 2 Mexican chorizo sausages, drained and sliced
- 1 smoked sausage, sliced
- 1 large onion, chopped
- 4 cloves garlic, minced
- 3 tomatoes, diced
- 1 tsp salt
- 1 tsp ground black pepper
- 3 bay leaves
- Water
- White rice, for serving
- Farofa, for serving

INSTRUCTIONS

1. Heat oil in a soup pot over medium heat. Add the bacon and cook until crisp. Then transfer to plate.
2. In the same pot, brown the ribs and sausages in batches. Set each aside as cooked. Add more oil if needed.
3. Heat oil in a pan, and add onion and garlic. Sauté for 5 minutes or until soft and translucent.
4. Stir in tomatoes and cook for 3 minutes.
5. Drain and rinse the soaked beans. Stir into the pot with the ribs, bacon, sausages, salt, pepper, and bay leaves. Cover the mixture with water (8 cups).
6. Bring to boil, cover and simmer for 2-2½ hours.
7. If you want to make it thicker then uncover and cook for another 20 minutes.
8. Serve with white rice and sprinkle some farofa on top.

Brigadeiros

There is a great Brazilian dessert that is like a bonbon and delicious called Brigadeiro. This is a great type of sweet that is loved in Brazil. Try this sweet dish!

 Serving: 24 pieces   **Time: 30 minutes**

INGREDIENTS

- 1 (14oz) can sweet condensed milk
- 4 tbsp cocoa powder, sifted
- 2 tbsp butter, plus more for rolling balls
- A pinch of salt
- Good quality chocolate sprinkle or your favorite

INSTRUCTIONS

1. Combine the sweet condensed milk, the cocoa powder, the salt and the butter in a saucepan. Heat it over medium-low.
2. Cook it, stirring constantly until it thickens. If it takes a while for the mixture to stir, then your Brigadeiro is ready. Allow to cool to room temperature.
3. Meanwhile, spread the sprinkles on a plate.
4. Grease your hands with butter and roll the brigadeiros into little balls.
5. Roll the brigadeiro balls on the sprinkles and place them on paper.

Moqueca

Moqueca is a simple dish of Brazil. It can make with your favorite fish and simmered in coconut milk with onion, tomatoes, chilies and lime. Easy, fast and full of flavor! You can serve this with rice!

INGREDIENTS

 Serving: 4   Time: 35 minutes

Fish:
- 1–1½ lb firm white fish, rinsed, pat dried, 2-inch pieces
- ½ tsp salt
- one lime- zest and juice

Stew/ Sauce:
- 2–3 tbsp coconut or olive oil
- 1 onion- finely diced
- ½ tsp salt
- 1 cup carrot, diced
- 1 red bell pepper, diced
- 4 garlic cloves, roughly chopped
- ½ jalapeno, finely diced
- 1 tbsp tomato paste
- 2 tsp paprika
- 1 tsp ground cumin
- 1 cup fish or chicken stock
- 1 ½ cups tomatoes, diced
- 1 14 oz can coconut milk
- Salt, to taste
- ½ cup chopped cilantro, scallions or Italian parsley
- Squeeze of lime

INSTRUCTIONS

1. In a bowl, combine the fish, salt, zest from half the lime and 1 tbsp lime juice. Toss to coat well. Set aside.
2. Heat the olive oil over medium in a pan. Add onion and salt, and sauté for 2-3 minutes.
3. Stir in carrot, bell pepper, garlic and jalapeno and cook for 4-5 more minutes.
4. Stir in tomato paste, spices and stock. Mix and bring to boil.
5. Add tomatoes, cover the pot with a lid and simmer gently on medium-low for 5 minutes or until tender.
6. Add the coconut milk and nestle the fish in the stew, Simmer gently for 5 minutes or until cooked through. Spoon the flavorful coconut broth over the fish and cook until desired thickness.
7. To serve, serve over rice, sprinkle with cilantro or scallions and a squeeze of lime.
8. Drizzle with a little olive oil and lemon juice.

Pão De Queijo

Pão de queijo is probably Brazil's most famous food recipe. Very similar to gougeres and pao de queijo is basically a pate a choux. Made with tapioca flour instead of wheat flour!

Serving: 20　　　**Time: 1 hour**

INGREDIENTS

- 1 cup whole milk
- 2 tbsp butter
- 2 tbsp neutral oil
- 3 cups sweet tapioca flour
- 1 tsp salt
- 2 eggs, beaten
- 4 oz grated cheese

INSTRUCTIONS

1. Preheat the oven to 400° F. Line a baking sheet with parchment paper
2. In a pot, add milk, butter and oil. Bring to boil.
3. In a bowl, combine tapioca flour and salt with a stand mixer.
4. Add hot milk and mix until smooth. Add the eggs and mix until fully incorporated (one egg at a time).
5. Add the cheese and mix well. If dough is too soft to scoop, refrigerate for 30 minutes.
6. Scoot out the dough and place on baking sheet on 1-inch distance.
7. Bake 20-25 minutes or until lightly golden (for crispy, bake for 25-30 minutes).
8. Eat warm right away or let cool.

Escondidinho De Carne

Delicious Escondidinho recipe made with shredded beef and meat broth topped with mashed potatoes and manioc. Delicious recipe of Brazil!

 Serving: 6   **Time: 40 minutes**

INGREDIENTS

- 3 tbsp unsalted butter
- Half a medium onion cut into rings
- 1 lb ground beef duckling
- ½ cup tomato pulp
- ½ cup chopped green olives
- 2 sachets red seasoning
- 2 pinches of salt
- 1¾ lb cassava, cooked and squeezed while still hot
- 1 cup milk
- ¼ lb grated mozzarella

INSTRUCTIONS

1. Melt the 1 tbsp butter in a saucepan over high heat. Sauté the onion for 2 minutes.
2. Stir in the ground beef and cook until brown or for 10 minutes, stirring occasionally.
3. Stir in the tomato pulp, olives, 1 sachet red seasoning and 1 pinch of salt. Mix and remove from heat.
4. Combine the manioc, milk, remaining butter, red seasoning and salt, and mix vigorously until a puree.
5. Preheat the oven to 350° F. Line a refractory (6x10 inch).
6. Place half of the puree on base of refractory. Place half of the mozzarella on top.
7. Top with ground beef and then remaining puree. Spread remaining mozzarella on top.
8. Bake for 10 minutes, or until the mozzarella melted.
9. Remove from the oven and serve immediately.

Ajiaco

This is a classic soup recipe of Colombian. You can serve it with cream, capers, avocado, mote and shredded chicken breast. Popular and delicious recipe of Colombia.

 Serving: 4   **Time: 1 hr 20 minutes**

INGREDIENTS

- 2 chicken breasts, skinless
- 2 cobs choclo corn
- 4 garlic cloves, sliced
- ½ white onion, diced
- 1 yellow pepper, diced
- 4 medium potatoes, peeled and diced
- 2 spring onions, chopped
- 12 papas criollas, cut in half
- 8 tbsp guascas
- Serve:
- 6 coriander sprigs, chopped,
- 100ml single or double cream
- 4 tbsp capers , drained
- 1 avocado, peeled, diced

INSTRUCTIONS

1. In a pan, combine the chicken, corn cobs, garlic, onion, pepper, potatoes, spring onions, coriander and 8 cups of water.
2. Bring to the boil, season well and simmer for 45 minutes over a medium heat.
3. Transfer the corn and the chicken to a plate.
4. Blend the remaining mixture with a hand blender until creamy.
5. Stir in the papas criollas and the guascas to the pan. Cook for about 10 minutes, or until the papas criollas are softened.
6. Shred the chicken breasts finely with your fingers, and slice the corn cobs.
7. In a bowl, place the chicken, corn cobs, cream, capers, avocado and extra chopped coriander.
8. Pour the soup into four soup bowls and serve.

Bandeja Paisa

Bandeja paisa is from Paisa region of Colombia and bandeja means platter. This delicious spread of crispy, fatty pork belly, hogao, saucy red beans, beef, chorizo, cheesy arepas, caramelized plantains, and fried eggs!

🕐 **Serving: 4**   👤 **Time: 13 hours**

INGREDIENTS

Chicharrones:
- 1 lb skinless pork belly
- 2 tsp kosher salt
- 2 tsp granulated sugar
- ½ tsp ground cumin

Hogao:
- ¼ cup canola oil
- 4 cups chopped yellow onions
- 1½ cups chopped green bell pepper
- 1 tbsp achiote paste
- 5 cups chopped plum tomatoes
- 5 garlic cloves, chopped
- 2 tsp ground cumin
- 1 ¾ tsp kosher salt
- ¼ cup chopped fresh cilantro

Frijoles Rojos:
- 1¾ cups dried large red beans, soaked in water over night
- 1 tbsp canola oil
- ¼ lb skinless pork belly, 1-in. pieces

- 8 cups lower-sodium chicken broth
- 2 cups Hogao
- 1 tsp ground cumin
- ¾ tsp kosher salt

Carne Molida:
- 1 tbsp canola oil
- 1 lb ground chuck
- 1 cup Hogao
- 1 tsp kosher salt
- ½ tsp ground cumin

Chorizo:
- 1 tbsp canola oil
- 4 (2½-oz) fresh Mexican chorizo links

Arepas:
- 1 cup (about 5 oz.) white masarepa (pre-cooked corn flour)
- 4 oz asadero cheese or queso blanco, shredded (about 1 cup)

- 1 cup warm water
- ¾ tsp kosher salt
- 3 tbsp canola oil, divided

Tajadas de platano:
- 2 large ripe plantains, peeled
- ¼ cup canola oil
- ¼ tsp kosher salt
- Huevos fritos:
- 2 tbsp canola oil
- 4 large eggs
- ¼ tsp kosher salt
- ⅛ tsp black pepper

Additional:
- 3 cups cooked white rice
- 2 avocados, halved
- Fresh cilantro leaves

Chicharrones:
1. In a rimmed baking sheet, add pork belly.
2. In a bowl, combine the salt, sugar and cumin. Pour to pork belly and rub well. Wrap pork in plastic wrap, and refrigerate for 6-12 hours.
3. Preheat oven to 425°F. Place the pork on a lightly greased wire rack. Place rack in a rimmed baking sheet, and bake for 30 minutes or until golden brown.
4. Reduce oven to 250°F, and cook for 1 hour and 15 minutes until pork is tender. Allow the pork to cool to room temperature. Wrap the pork and refrigerate for an hour.
5. Cut pork into 4 strips (¾ inch).
6. Cook the pork in a skillet for 4 minutes or until golden brown.

Hogao:
7. In a skillet, heat oil over medium. Add onions, bell pepper, and achiote paste. Sauté for 8 minutes.
8. Stir in tomatoes, garlic, cumin, and salt. Cook for 15 minutes. Remove from heat, and stir in cilantro.

Frijoles Rojos:
9. Soak the beans overnight and then drain the beans.
10. In a Dutch oven, heat oil. Add pork belly and cook for 8 minutes or until brown, stirring occasionally.
11. Stir in beans, broth, Hogao, cumin, and salt. Bring to a boil and simmer until beans are tender, for 4½ -5 hours, stirring occasionally. Add more water if the mixture is too thick.
12. Carne Molida:
13. In a skillet, heat oil. Add beef and cook until brown, stirring to break into pieces, until browned, 6-8 minutes.
14. Stir in Hogao, salt, and cumin. Cook for 2 minutes.

Chorizo:
15. In a skillet, heat oil. Cook chorizo links for 15 minutes turning occasionally.

Arepas:
16. In a bowl, mix the masarepa, cheese, water, salt, and 1 tbsp of the oil until smooth. Cover and let rest for 10 minutes.
17. Shape the dough into 4 medium balls. Gently roll each ball into a ½ inch-thick disk.
18. Heat the remaining 2 tbsp oil in a large cast-iron skillet over medium. Cook arepas for 5 minutes per side until golden brown.

Tajadas de Plátano:
19. Cut plantains into ½-inch-thick slices.
20. In a skillet, heat oil over medium. Cook plantains for 2 minutes on each side or until golden brown in batches. Transfer to a plate lined with paper towels, and sprinkle with salt.

Huevos Fritos:
21. In a nonstick skillet, heat oil. Add eggs and sprinkle with salt and pepper. Cook for 4-5 minutes.
22. In the 4 serving platters, evenly divide Chicharrones, Frijoles Rojos, Carne Molida, Chorizo, Arepas, Tajadas de Plátano, Huevos Fritos, rice, avocados, and remaining Hogao. Garnish with cilantro.

Pan de Bono

Pandebono is traditional Colombian cheese bread. This bread is perfect and delicious. You can serve it as a side dish. This is favorite of Colombian kids.

 Serving: 4   Time: 35 minutes

INGREDIENTS

- ⅔ cup cassava starch or yuca flour
- ¼ cup precooked cornmeal
- 1 cup Colombian quesito
- 1 + ¼ cup feta cheese
- 1 large egg

INSTRUCTIONS

1. Preheat the oven to 400°F. Line a baking sheet with parchment paper.
2. Add the yuca flour, cheese and masarepa in a food processor. Process until mix.
3. Add the egg slowly during processing.
4. Divide the mixture into 12 equal size portions, shaping them into balls and place on a prepared baking sheet.
5. Bake for about 15-20 minutes or until golden. Serve warm.

Cocadas

Cocadas are coconut dessert from Colombia. These soft, chewy coconut mounds are mixed with dulche de leche and studded with macadamia nuts. This is like macaroons, but much more delicious!

 Serving: 24 cookies   **Time: 1hour**

INGREDIENTS

- 3½ cups shredded sweetened coconut
- ¾ cup sweetened condensed milk
- 2½ tbsp cornstarch
- ½ tsp almond extract
- 1 tsp vanilla extract
- ¼ cup confectioners' sugar, optional

INSTRUCTIONS

1. Preheat oven to 400° F. Line a cookie sheet with parchment paper.
2. In a bowl, combine coconut, cornstarch, condensed milk, almond extract, and vanilla extract. Rest for 3 to 5 minutes.
3. Drop a spoonful of the mixture on the cookie sheet by 2 tbsp spoon on 1 inch distance.
4. Bake for 15-20 minutes until lightly golden brown. Remove from oven and allow to cool on wire rack.
5. Dust with confectioners' sugar.

Lechona

Colombians love to cook this dish during the holidays. Lechona is also known as a stuffed roasted pig. Lechona is made year-round, especially at different restaurants and even grocery.

 Serving: 6   Time: 3 hours

INGREDIENTS

- 2 lb pork fatback skins, rinsed and pat dried
- ¼ cup pork fat
- 4 scallions chopped
- 4 garlic cloves finely chopped
- 1 tsp ground cumin
- 1 tsp sazon with azafran
- ¾ cup peas
- 1¼ cups cooked white rice
- Salt and pepper
- 2 lb pork meat cut into small pieces

INSTRUCTIONS

1. Melt the pork fat in a saucepan. Add the scallions and garlic. Sauté for about 3 minutes.
2. Combine the pork meat, cooked rice, ground cumin, sazon, peas, salt and pepper in a bowl. Mix well.
3. Add the scallion mixture to the bowl. Cover and place in the refrigerator for 1 hour.
4. Place the pork fat skin on a baking sheet lined with foil. Place rice mixture on top.
5. Roll the pork skin to cover the rice and pork mixture. Tie to hold with kitchen string.
6. Preheat the oven to 475° F.
7. Bake for 40 minutes uncovered to allow the skin to brown. Cover with foil and cook for about 45 minutes. Then remove from heat and allow to cool.
8. Place the pork on cutting board. Carve the lechona.
9. Serve with arepa, salted potatoes and lime wedges on the side.

Ceviche

Ceviche is a famous dish from Peru, where fresh seafood is "cooked" in lime juice and mixed with chili, cilantro, onion and other flavorings. It's bursting with flavor and perfectly refreshing.

Serving: 6   Time: 50 minutes

INGREDIENTS

- 1¼ lb shrimp, peeled, deveined and tails removed
- 1/3 cup fresh lime juice
- 1/3 cup fresh lemon juice
- 1 cup diced roma tomatoes
- ¾ cup chopped red onion
- ½ cup chopped cilantro
- 1 medium jalapeno pepper, diced
- Salt and pepper, to taste
- 1 cup diced cucumber
- 1 medium avocado, diced

INSTRUCTIONS

1. In a pot, bring water to boil. Add shrimp and cook until pink or for a minute.
2. Meanwhile, add ice water in a bowl. Transfer the cooked shrimp water to ice water.
3. Allow to cool for 5 minutes. Then drain and chop the shrimp into ½ inch pieces
4. In a bowl, mix the shrimp, lime juice, lemon juice, tomatoes, onion, cilantro and jalapeno pepper. Season with salt and pepper, to taste.
5. Refrigerate for ½-1 hour.
6. Add cucumber and avocado. Then serve.

Lomo Saltado

This is a simple and delicious dish. Tender slices of deeply seared beef, onions, tomatoes, and crispy fried potatoes unite in this traditional Peru stir-fry.

 Serving: 4   **Time: 40 minutes**

INGREDIENTS

- 11 oz thick potato slices
- 18 oz sirloin steak, cubed
- 1 tsp cumin ground
- Salt, to taste
- 4 tbsp plain vinegar
- 2 tbsp olive oil
- 1 tsp black pepper, freshly crushed
- 4 tbsp soy sauce
- 1 red onion, sliced
- 1 ají amarillo chili pepper, finely sliced
- 1 tsp fresh garlic paste
- ½ cup beef stock
- 2 tomatoes, sliced
- 20 oz white rice cooked
- Handful cilantro leaves
- ¼ tsp oregano ground

INSTRUCTIONS

1. Heat oil in a pan, add potato and cook until fried.
2. In a bowl, combine the sirloin steak, cumin, salt, vinegar, 1 tbsp olive oil, black pepper and the soy sauce. Toss to coat and let rest for 10 minutes.
3. In a wok, heat the remaining olive oil. Add steaks and cook for 5 minutes.
4. Stir in the onion, ají amarillo chili pepper and the garlic paste. Cook for a minute and stir continuously.
5. Add the beef stock and tomato. Cook for 30 seconds.
6. Stir in the ground oregano and fried potatoes. Toss for 10 seconds.
7. Serve immediately with white rice and garnish with a few cilantro leaves.

Aji De Gallina

This is a delicious, traditional Peruvian chicken stew in a spicy, nutty cheese sauce. It takes time, but is well worth it! I serve this over boiled white rice and baby yellow potatoes.

 Serving: 4   **Time: 1 hr 10 minutes**

INGREDIENTS

- 1¼ lb chicken breast
- 2½ cups chicken stock
- 3½ tbsp of oil
- 1 large onion, chopped
- 4 garlic cloves, minced
- 1 pinch of ground cumin
- 1 pinch of turmeric
- 1 tbsp aji amarillo paste
- 5 slices of bread, crusts removed
- 60g of walnuts, toasted and ground
- 50g of Parmesan, grated
- ¾ cup of evaporated milk
- Salt and pepper
- To serve:
- 4 eggs, hard-boiled
- 60g of olives
- 4 potatoes, peeled and boiled
- Cooked brown rice, cooked

INSTRUCTIONS

1. Poach the chicken breasts in the chicken stock for 20 minutes. Drain, shred and reserve.
2. Heat oil in a saucepan. Add the onion, garlic, turmeric, cumin and aji amarillo paste. Sauté until golden.
3. Soak the bread 2 cups of the stock from the poached chicken.
4. In a blender, add soaked bread and blend for 2 minutes and then transfer to onion mixture.
5. Cook slowly for 10 minutes, stirring until slightly thickened
6. Stir in the chopped walnuts, grated Parmesan and shredded chicken. Cook until thickened.
7. Add evaporated milk, 5 minutes before serving. Cook over low heat and adjust the salt.
8. Serve with boiled rice, halved potatoes, eggs and olives.

Papas a La Huancaina

Papas a la Huancaina mean Huancainan-style potato. An easy recipe of sliced potatoes with a special sauce comes from Huancayo Peru. You can serve it as a side dish.

 Serving: 4   **Time: 40 minutes**

INGREDIENTS

- ½ cup aji amarillo paste
- 2 tbsp vegetable oil
- 1 cup evaporated milk
- 4 soda crackers
- 8 oz queso fresco
- Salt
- Iceberg lettuce leaves
- 6 yellow potatoes
- Black olives
- 3 hard-boiled eggs, sliced
- Parsley sprigs

INSTRUCTIONS

1. In a pot, boil the potatoes in water. Peel them and slices them thicker.
2. In a blender, add the aji amarillo paste, oil, milk, crackers, queso fresco and salt. Process until smooth.
3. In four serving plates, place lettuce leaves on each. Add potato slices, and cover with a few tbsp of the blended sauce.
4. Garnish with black olives, hard-boiled eggs and parsley. Serve immediately.

Peruvian Causa

This dish with layered with potato and meat. You are going to love this dish! Make the layer of potato and meat thin or thick, it's up to you. You can replace the tuna with chicken or other fish.

🕐 Serving: 4   👤 Time: 35 minutes

INGREDIENTS

Potato Layer:
- 2 lb potatoes, peeled
- ¼ cup olive oil
- ¼ cup lime juice
- 1-2 tbsp aji amarillo paste
- salt and pepper, to taste

Filling:
- 2 pouches tuna
- 3 tbsp mayonnaise
- 1 tsp lime juice
- 2 tbsp red onion, finely diced
- 1 tbsp fresh parsley, minced
- 1 ripe avocado, sliced

INSTRUCTIONS

1. In a bowl, mix the tuna, mayonnaise, lime juice, onion and parsley. Season with salt and pepper to taste. Cover the bowl and refrigerate.
2. In a pot, add potatoes and cover with salted water. Bring to boil and cook until fork-tender. Then drain and mash them. Allow to cool.
3. In a bowl, combine the cooled mashed potatoes, olive oil, lime juice and aji amarillo paste. Season with salt and pepper to taste.
4. Line a casserole dish with plastic wrap. Fill 1/3 of the dish with mixture.
5. Top a layer of sliced avocado, then a layer of tuna salad. Finally, top the casserole dish with another layer of potato.
6. Wrap the dish with plastic wrap and refrigerate for 30 minutes.
7. Flip the causa onto a plate and remove the plastic wrap. Garnish with a sprig of parsley and serve cold.

Ropa Vieja

This is a famous dish in Cuba and popular throughout the Latin Caribbean. A combination of shredded beef in a rich, delicious and flavorful sauce of tomatoes, onions, bell peppers, and spices!

INGREDIENTS

- 2 lb chuck or flank steak
- 1 large yellow onion thinly sliced
- 1 of each large green, red and yellow bell pepper, thinly sliced
- 4 cloves garlic minced
- 2 tsp dried oregano
- 2 tsp ground cumin
- 2 tsp sweet paprika
- 1 tsp smoked paprika
- 1/8 tsp ground allspice
- 1/8 tsp ground cloves
- 2 tsp kosher salt
- ½ tsp freshly ground black pepper
- ½ cup dry white wine
- 1 cup chicken broth
- 1 (16 oz) can crushed tomatoes
- 1 (6 oz) can tomato paste
- 2 bay leaves
- 1 large carrot, cut in half
- 1 large stalk celery, cut in half
- 1 cup green olives, rinsed and drained
- ½ cup roasted red peppers, drained
- ¼ cup pimientos, drained
- 2 tbsp capers, rinsed and drained
- 1/3 cup chopped fresh parsley

 Serving: 8　　　 **Time: 5 hours**

INSTRUCTIONS

1. Place the beef on paper towel and let pat dry the beef. Then sprinkle with salt and black pepper.
2. In a Dutch oven, heat oil over high heat. Add beef and cook until brown. Then transfer to a plate.
3. Add the onion and bell peppers to the pot and cook for 15-20 minutes over medium heat.
4. Stir in the garlic and spices and cook for a minute. Pour the white wine and bring to boil.
5. Pour the broth, crushed tomatoes, tomato paste and bay leaves. Simmer for 5 minutes.
6. Add cooked beef and cover the pot and simmer until tender for 3-4 hours over low heat. Remove the celery, carrots and bay leaves.
7. Transfer the beef to a bowl and shred it with a fork. Return the shredded beef to the pot.
8. Add the olives, roasted red peppers, capers and pimientos.
9. Simmer until thicken or for 30 minutes. Stir in the parsley and add salt and pepper to taste.

Lechon Asado

Lechon Asado is also known as Cuban roast pork, marinated in a flavorful homemade garlic-citrus marinade and slow-roasted to perfection!

Serving: 6   Time: 3 hours

INGREDIENTS

- 3 lb boneless pork shoulder roast, pat dried
- ½ cup orange juice
- ¼ cup lime juice
- ¼ cup lemon juice
- 1½ tsp dry oregano
- 1 tsp ground cumin
- 1½ tsp salt
- 8 cloves garlic crushed
- 1 small onion, sliced
- Ground pepper, to taste

INSTRUCTIONS

1. Prepare a plastic container or freezer bag. Add the orange juice, lime juice, lemon juice, oregano, cumin, salt, garlic, onion and pepper. Mix well.
2. Add the pork and seal the bag. Shake to coat well. Refrigerate overnight, turn the bag at least once.
3. Remove the pork from fridge 1 hour before cooking. Allow coming to room temperature.
4. Preheat the oven to 325° F.
5. In a roasting dish, place the pork with some marinade juice (skin side up).
6. Baste the pork with the juice in the dish after 1-2 hr and continue cooking. Roast for 3 hours.
7. Meanwhile, in a pan, add the remaining marinade. Bring to boil and simmer for 5 minutes. Serve it as a sauce with the pork.

Yuca Con Mojo

This is tender, creamy cassava, drizzled with a citrus garlic sauce. Yuca con Mojo is one of the most traditional dishes of Cuban food. You can serve it as a side dish.

Serving: 4   Time: 35 minutes

INGREDIENTS

- 1½ lb yuca, 1-inch chunks
- 2 large red onions, sliced
- ¼ cup fresh orange juice, zest for garnish
- ¼ cup fresh lime juice
- 1 tbsp chopped cilantro
- 6 cloves garlic, minced
- ¼ cup olive oil
- ½ tsp dried oregano
- ¼ tsp ground cumin
- Kosher salt, to taste
- Freshly ground black pepper, to taste

INSTRUCTIONS

1. In a saucepan, add yuca and cover with salted water. Bring to heat and boil for 30 minutes or until tender. Then drain and place in a serving dish. Cover the dish and set aside
2. In a bowl, onions, orange juice, lime juice, cilantro, and garlic in a bowl. Pour the mixture over yuka.
3. In a pan, heat the olive oil, oregano, cumin, salt, and pepper for a minute. Pour over yuca.
4. Garnish with cilantro leaves and orange zest.

Cuban Sandwich

A Cuban sandwich, known as a Cubano, is a grilled ham-and-cheese sandwich variation that was created in Florida by Cuban immigrants who needed a filling and easy-to-carry lunch.

🕐 **Serving: 2**   👤 **Time: 30 minutes**

INGREDIENTS

- ¼ cup mayonnaise and mustard
- A pinch of cayenne pepper
- 8 oz loaf Cuban bread
- 8 slices swiss cheese
- 6 thin slices of cooked ham
- 1 ½ cups cooked pork
- 1 large dill pickle
- 2 tbsp of butter

INSTRUCTIONS

1. Mix mayonnaise, mustard, and cayenne together in a bowl to make the sauce.
2. Cut the Cuban bread loaf into two halves for making 2 sandwiches.
3. Mix the mustard and mayonnaise with cayenne pepper and spread them on both sides of the sandwiches.
4. Place the Swiss cheese and ham slices over the sandwiches.
5. Now add the cooked pork along with the pickle slices and then again add the Swiss cheese slices.
6. Grab a griller or toaster and toast the sandwiches to give them a good crisp for about 5 minutes.

Picadillo a la Habanera

Picadillo a la habanera is a dish cook in Havana and a traditional recipe of Cuba. Its ingredients came from all over the world, but the mixture of them, to achieve this delicious flavor, was born in the capital of Cuba.

 Serving: 4   **Time: 30 minutes**

INGREDIENTS

- 5 tbsp oil
- 1 potato, peeled and diced, soaked in salted water and drained
- ½ pepper, chopped
- 1 onion, finely chopped
- 4 cloves of garlic, minced
- 1 lb picadillo
- ¼ cup red wine
- Salt
- ½ cup tomato puree
- ½ tsp cumin
- ½ tsp ground oregano
- 1 bay leaf
- A pinch red pepper powder
- Green olives
- Parsley and raisins

INSTRUCTIONS

1. In a pan, heat oil and add the potatoes. Cook until golden brown. Remove the cooked potatoes from pan.
2. Add the peppers, onion and garlic to the pan. Sauté for 2 minutes or until softened.
3. Stir in the picadillo and cook for 5-8 minutes. Add the 60 ml of red wine.
4. Turn heat to high and add the salt. Cook until wine evaporated.
5. Lower the heat. Stir in tomato puree, cumin, oregano, 1 bay leaf and a pinch of powdered red pepper. Cook for 5 minutes.
6. Add the green olives, raisins and the cooked potato.
7. Garnish with a little chopped parsley and voila before serving.

Mofongo

Mofongo is served mostly in Puerto Rico. Mofongo is deep-fried green plantains mashed together with pork or chicharron or seafood such as shrimp.

🕐 **Serving: 2**   👤 **Time: 20 minutes**

INGREDIENTS

- 5 green plantains, peeled and sliced(1½")
- 1 lb chicharrón
- 4 cloves garlic, minced
- 4 tsp olive oil
- 2 cups oil

INSTRUCTIONS

1. Soak the plantains in salty water for 15 minutes. Drain them and transfer to a dish lined with a paper towel and dry well.
2. In a skillet, heat the oil. Add plantains and cook until they turn golden brown. Drain on a paper towel.
3. Mash the plantains while slowly pouring the olive oil by using a mortar and pestle.
4. Add the garlic and the pieces of chicharrón. Crush again with the pestle.
5. Divide the mixture into 4 pieces. Mold them into the shape of a half-sphere using your hands.
6. Serve hot with your favorite meat.

Arroz Con Gandules

Arroz Con Gandules is a flavorful and traditional rice dish in Puerto Rico. It is usually served during Christmas. You can serve it as a main dish.

⏱ **Serving: 8**　　　👤 **Time: 30 minutes**

INGREDIENTS

- 1 tbsp olive oil
- 1/3 cup country ham or bacon, diced
- 1/3 cup sofrito
- 3 cups low sodium chicken broth
- 1½ tsp sazón con achiote y culantro
- 1 cube chicken bouillon
- 2 tbsp tomato paste
- 1 tsp dried Italian seasoning
- ¼ cup fresh cilantro, chopped
- 2-3 bay leaves
- 2 tbsp pimento-stuffed olives, optional
- 15 oz can pigeon peas, drained and rinsed
- 2 cups parboiled rice

INSTRUCTIONS

1. Heat olive oil in a Dutch oven. Add the bacon and sofrito. Stir in cook for 4 minutes or until brown.
2. Stir in the Sazon, tomato sauce or paste and chicken bouillon. Stir to combine.
3. Stir in the drained pigeon peas, Italian seasoning or oregano, bay leaves, broth, cilantro and olives.
4. Bring to boil and taste and adjust salt. Add the rice. Stir to mix well. Cover and continue cooking until liquid is absorbed.
5. Stir the rice, and cover again. Lower the flame to low, and allow it to steam for 20-25 minutes.

Bistec Encebollado

Bistec encebollado is a traditional dish of Puerto Rican, flavoring-packed combo of onions, sofrito and vinegar, before being stewed in a savory tomato-based sauce.

Serving: 4   Time: 5 hours

INGREDIENTS

- 2 lb beef steak, sliced
- ½ cup olive oil
- 2 tbsp minced garlic
- Dash of dried oregano leaves
- 2 large white onions, sliced in rings
- ¼ cup distilled white vinegar
- ¼ cup sofrito
- 1 ½ cups water
- 1 tsp salt

INSTRUCTIONS

1. In a gallon-sized plastic bag, put all the ingredients and mix them. Refrigerate for 4-24 hours.
2. Then transfer the mixture to a skillet. Bring to boil and simmer over low heat for 30-40 minutes or until meat is tender.

Pernil

A traditional Latin American dish, also known as Roast Pork Shoulder, Pernil is marinated overnight and roasted until fall-apart tender. Juicy and delicious, it is an easy yet impressive centerpiece for your Christmas table!

Serving: 8   Time: 4 hr 10 minutes

INGREDIENTS

- 2 large onions, chunks
- 3 cloves garlic, peeled
- Juice of 4 limes
- 1½ cup white wine
- Kosher salt, to taste
- Freshly ground black pepper, to taste
- 1 whole (4-8 lb) pork shoulder, bone-in, skin-on
- 2 tbsp fresh thyme leaves
- 2 tbsp fresh rosemary
- ¼ cup butter, softened

INSTRUCTIONS

1. In a blender, blend the onions, garlic, lime juice, 1 cup white wine, salt and pepper together until smooth. Add more wine if the mixture is thick. Set aside.
2. Score the skin on the pork shoulder by making the cross.
3. In a bowl, add the pork and onion mixture. Sprinkle with the herbs and rub the mixture into the pork, coat well. Cover with plastic and refrigerate for 12-24 hours, turning a few times.
4. Preheat the oven to 350° F.
5. In a roasting pan, add the pork with marinade with wine. Roast for 35-40 minutes or until tender. Remove from oven.
6. Turn the pork, skin side up, coat with the butter and place it under the broiler until crisp.
7. Let cool and serve.

Pastelon

This is a traditional dish of Puerto Rican, made with layers of thinly-sliced plantains, ground beef, and cheese! Pastelon is look like lasagna. It's the perfect casserole to cook for a family.

🕐 Serving: 4   👤 Time: 1 hr 45 minutes

INGREDIENTS

- 1 bunch fresh cilantro
- 1 bunch fresh culantro
- 1 red bell pepper, chopped
- 1 green bell pepper, chopped
- Cloves of 1 head garlic, peeled
- 1 tsp dried oregano
- ½ tsp ground cumin
- 1¼ cups canola oil, divided
- 5 pimento-stuffed spanish olives, sliced

- 1 lb ground beef
- ½ tsp kosher salt
- 2 tsp dried adobo seasoning, divided
- 1 ¼ tsp sazon goya seasoning powder
- 1 can tomato sauce
- 4 very ripe plantains, peeled and sliced lengthwise
- 3 cups shredded mozzarella cheese, divided
- 2 large eggs

INSTRUCTIONS

1. In a food processor, place the cilantro, culantro, onion, red and green bell peppers, garlic, oregano, and cumin. Pulse until combined.
2. In a pan, heat ¼ cups oil, and sauté the sofrito for 3 minutes until brown. Stir in the olives.
3. Stir in the ground beef and cook for 7 minutes until no longer pink. Season with salt.
4. Stir in the 1 tsp adobo seasoning, the Sazón seasoning and the tomato sauce. Cook for 5 minutes.
5. Transfer the beef mixture to a bowl, discarding any excess liquid.
6. Wipe out the pan with a towel and heat the remaining oil over medium-high heat. Add the plantains and fry for 4-5 minutes until light brown on the edges, in batches. Then transfer to a plate lined with a paper towel. Season on both sides with salt.
7. Preheat the oven to 350°F.
8. In a 8-inch square baking dish, place a single layer of plantains. Top with half of the meat mixture.
9. Sprinkle with 1 cup of mozzarella on top. Repeat with more plantains, the remaining meat sauce, and another cup of mozzarella. Finish with the remaining plantains.
10. Mix the eggs and remaining adobo seasoning in a bowl. Beat well.
11. Pour the egg mixture over the plantains, then cover the baking dish with foil.
12. Bake for 25 minutes or until cheese is bubbly.
13. Remove from the oven and turn the oven to broil. Uncover the dish and sprinkle the remaining cup of mozzarella over the top. Broil for 5 minutes.
14. Allow to cool for 10 minutes and serve.

Baleadas

This is the most popular dish in Honduras. Just top the tortillas as you desire - refried beans, fried eggs, chorizo, cheese or avocado. The possibilities are endless.

 Serving: 8   **Time: 50 minutes**

INGREDIENTS

Tortillas:
- 2 cups all-purpose flour
- 1 cup water
- ½ cup vegetable oil
- 1 egg
- ½ tsp salt

Filling:
- 2 cups refried beans, warmed
- 1 avocado, sliced
- ½ cup crumbled fresh white cheese
- ¼ cup (fresh cream)

INSTRUCTIONS

1. In a bowl, combine the flour, water, vegetable oil, egg, and salt. Knead the mixture until smooth and no longer sticky.
2. Form the dough into 8 medium balls. Cover and let rest for 20 minutes.
3. Stretch each ball of dough into a thick tortilla.
4. Heat oil in a skillet. Cook each tortilla for a minute on each side or until browned.
5. Layer refried beans, avocado, and queso fresco over tortillas. Drizzle crema on top; fold tortillas in half overfilling.

Pan De Coco

Pan de coco is also known as coconut bread. It is dairy-free bread from Honduras. You can serve it alongside a main dish like curry or as a snack.

🕐 **Serving: 12 rolls**   👤 **Time: 3 hr 15 minutes**

INGREDIENTS

- ¼ cup warm water
- 1 tsp sugar
- 2¼ tsp active dry yeast
- 3¼ cup all-purpose flour
- ¼ cup sugar
- 2 tsp salt
- 1 cup coconut milk
- 2 tbsp coconut oil

INSTRUCTIONS

1. In a bowl, combine the water, yeast and sugar. Mix to dissolve.
2. In a large bowl, combine the flour, sugar, salt, coconut milk, coconut oil, and yeast mixture. Mix with stand mixer for 2 minutes. Push the mixture down from sides of bowl.
3. Knead for 5 minutes at this same speed until the dough is smooth, elastic and sticky to touch.
4. In a lightly greased bowl, place the dough and turn the dough over once to grease the top. Cover with a towel and keep warm for1-2 hours or until the dough doubles in size.
5. Place the dough on a floured surface and divide into 12 parts. Roll each and shape into a ball.
6. In a greased 9×13 inch baking pan, place the rolls in a prepared baking pan, cover with a towel and let them rise for 30 minutes.
7. Preheat oven to 375° F. Bake for 20-25 minutes or until golden brown on top.
8. Let them cool in the pan for 5 minutes.

Sopa De Caracol

This is a classic Honduran soup, is one of the popular Latin dish. There are many variations of the delicious soup for seafood that is widely consumed across Latin America.

 Serving: 8   **Time: 50 minutes**

INGREDIENTS

- 3 lb cassava, sliced
- 3 (1½ oz) cans coconut milk
- 3 lb conch
- 4 green bananas, sliced
- 3 white onions, chopped
- 4 carrots, sliced
- 3 green hot peppers, chopped
- 4 cloves garlic, crushed
- 7 tbsp margarine
- 1 large green bell pepper, chopped
- 1 bunch cilantro
- 3 cubes chicken consommé
- 3 tbsp achiote oil
- 1 bunch of Chinese cilantro
- 1½ cup milk
- 1½ cup water
- Salt and Pepper to taste

INSTRUCTIONS

1. Remove the flesh gently from the conch, then soften it thoroughly using the mallet.
2. Cut the flesh of the conch into 2 inches squares. Set it aside.
3. In a Dutch oven, melt the margarine over medium-high. Add the onions and cook for 2 minutes.
4. Stir in the bell peppers, garlic and hot peppers. Cook for 3 minutes.
5. Stir in the cubes of chicken consommé, carrots, and cassava. Sauté for 5 minutes.
6. Stir in the coconut milk, water and milk. Mix well, cover and cook for 20 minutes over medium heat.
7. Add the bananas, salt, pepper and annatto oil, mix and cook for eight minutes.
8. Stir in the conchs, cilantro and cilantro and mix.

Yuca Con Chicharrón

Yuca con chicharrón is a traditional dish of Honduras cook with cassava and fried pork rind. You can serve with chimol sauce and coleslaw.

🕐 **Serving: 4**

🧍 **Time: 1 hr 15 minutes**

INGREDIENTS

- ½ head green cabbage, finely shredded
- 2 plum tomatoes, finely diced
- ½ small white onion, minced
- ½ cup cider vinegar
- Kosher salt
- 2 lb frozen yucca
- ½ lb chicharrones, bite-sized pieces

For chicharrónes:
- 1 lb pork belly, skin on
- Water
- Salt and pepper, to taste
- Spices of choice like cayenne, sugar, and paprika
- 2 tsp baking soda

INSTRUCTIONS

For yucca:
1. Combine the cabbage, tomatoes, onion, and vinegar in a bowl.
2. Season with salt and vinegar, to taste. Refrigerate until needed
3. In a saucepan, add yucca and cover with cold water. Add 1 tbsp salt. Bring to boil and simmer over low heat for about 40 minutes or until fork-tender.
4. Drain the yucca, and slice into lengthwise pieces. Remove and discard the woody strip in the centre.
5. Return to pot, and cover to keep warm.

For chicharrónes:
6. In a bowl, place the pork. Combine the salt and baking soda, and rub on the skin. Then refrigerator for 1-24 hours. Then rinse with cold water and pat dry.
7. Cut the meat into 1-inch pieces and place into a wok. Cover the meat with water. Cook over low heat for about 3 hours. Flip the pork pieces every half an hour.
8. When only liquid fat remains, turn the heat to high and deep fry the lard for 3-5 minutes carefully.
9. Transfer the chicharrones to a plate lined with paper towels with the help of a spoon. Toss with salt and seasonings.
10. Distribute yucca evenly among plates and top with slaw and chicharrónes. Serve immediately.

Tamales

A Simple and delicious recipe of Honduras! Filled the Tamales with pork, chicken or beans and cheese! You can serve it as a side dish.

 Serving: 8   Time: 3 hours

INGREDIENTS

- 1 (4 lb) pack masa harina, divided
- 1 tomato, chopped
- 1 green bell pepper, chopped
- 1 onion, chopped
- 1 cup chopped fresh cilantro
- ¼ cup ground cumin
- 2 cubes chicken bouillon
- Salt, to taste
- 1 (6 oz) can tomato paste
- 3 cups vegetable oil
- 30 banana leaves, cut into 12x15 inch rectangles
- 3½ lb cubed cooked pork
- 3 large potatoes, peeled and cubed
- 2 cups cooked white rice
- 1 (15 oz) can peas, drained
- kitchen twine

INSTRUCTIONS

1. In a large pot, add ¾ the masa harina and water in batches, mixing to thin batter forms.
2. In a blender, put the tomato, green bell pepper, onion, cilantro, cumin, and bouillon. Blend until smooth.
3. Then transfer the blended mixture to the pot with the batter. Season with salt.
4. In a small pot, add about 5 cups of mixture. Stir in tomato paste and mix well.
5. In a large pot, 2 cups of oil into the large pot with batter and 1 cup of oil into the smaller pot with red batter.
6. Bring both pots to a boil, stirring continuously. Cook for 3-5 minutes or until flavors set. Remove from heat.
7. On the banana leaves, spoon 1 cup from large pot batter and ¼ cup red batter into the center of each.
8. Add small amounts of pork, potatoes, rice, and peas. Fold leaf over the filling several times; fold sides in. Wrap twine around the tamale to hold in place.
9. In a large pot, place the tamales and cover halfway with water.
10. Cover the pot with lid and cook over medium heat for 1 hour or until filling has thickened.

Birria Tacos

Rich and flavorful this birria is perfect served as a stew topped with onion, cilantro and a squeeze of fresh lime juice. OR chop up the meat and fry up some Quesabirria tacos! These are the most FAMOUS Tacos!

INGREDIENTS

- 1.5 lb beef shank
- 1 lb sirloin steak, cubed

Marinade:
- 3 dried guajillo peppers
- 1 can chipotle peppers in adobo
- ¼ cup vinegar
- ½ cup crushed tomatoes
- 5 cloves garlic
- 1 tsp dried oregano
- ½ tsp smoked paprika
- 1 tsp cumin

Stew:
- 1 medium onion chopped
- 1 cinnamon stick
- 2 bay leaves
- 6 whole cloves
- 1-quart chicken stock

Tacos:
- 12 (4-inch) corn or flour tortillas
- 1 medium onion, chopped
- 1 bunch cilantro, chopped
- 1 cup Mexican cheese, grated

 Serving: 4   **Time: 2 hours**

INSTRUCTIONS

1. Soak the guajillo peppers for 15 minutes in boiling water. Then drain and cut with scissor and remove the seeds.
2. In a bowl, season the sirloin with salt and pepper. Set aside.
3. In a blender, put all the marinade ingredients. Blend until a smooth paste and transfer to bowl with meat. Marinate for 2 hours to overnight.
4. Heat 2 tbsp oil in a skillet over medium heat. Sauté the onions for 6 minutes or until golden.
5. Stir in the meats, marinade, bay leaves, cinnamon sticks, cloves and chicken broth. Bring to boil and simmer for 45 minutes or until meat is tender.
6. Remove the meat. Shred and discard the bones.
7. Warm-up some tortillas and add in the stew.
8. Build your tacos, top with taco ingredients, then fry over medium heat on a nonstick skillet. Enjoy immediately with a margarita.

Chimichangas and Guacamole

Tucson is generally credited as the original home of the chimichanga. Filled with meat, onions and chiles!

 Serving: 6   **Time: 30 minutes**

INGREDIENTS

For the Chimichangas:
- 2 tbsp olive oil
- 2 cloves garlic, minced
- ¼ red onion, diced
- ½ poblano pepper, diced
- ½ jalapeño, seeded and diced
- 2 chicken breasts, cooked and shredded
- ¼ cup salsa, extra for serving
- 4 oz cheddar cheese, grated
- 14 (6-inches) flour tortilla
- 1 tbsp butter, melted
- Lime wedges
- Fresh cilantro

For the Guacamole:
- 2 avocados, peeled and pitted
- ¼ cup chopped cilantro
- 1 tbsp lime juice
- ½ tsp garlic powder
- ½ tsp ground cayenne pepper

INSTRUCTIONS

1. Preheat the oven to 400°F. Line a baking sheet with parchment paper.
2. Heat olive oil in a pan over medium-high heat.
3. Pour in the garlic, red onion, poblano, and jalapeño. Cook until softened for about 5 minutes.
4. Season with salt and pepper to taste.
5. In a bowl, combine the pepper mixture, shredded chicken, salsa, and cheese.
6. Warm the tortillas in the microwave for 30 seconds.
7. Fill the bottom of each tortilla with 2 tbsp of the filling. Roll the tortilla over the filling tightly.
8. Place seam-side down on the baking sheet. Brush with melted butter on top.
9. Bake for 20 minutes. Remove from oven and serve with guacamole.

Chilaquiles

Make Mexican chilaquiles by simmering fried corn tortillas in salsa and serving with cheese, eggs, or beans. An easy and filling breakfast of Mexico!

 Serving: 4   **Time: 30 minutes**

INGREDIENTS

- 12 corn tortillas, preferably stale, or left out overnight to dry out a bit, quartered or cut into 6 wedges
- Corn oil
- Salt
- 2 cups red chili sauce or salsa
- A few sprigs of epazote, optional

Garnishes:
- Cotija cheese or queso fresco
- Crema Mexicana
- Cilantro, chopped
- 1 red onion, chopped
- Avocado, sliced or roughly chopped

INSTRUCTIONS

1. Heat oil in a pan over medium heat. Fry the tortillas until golden brown.
2. Line a plate with a paper towel and transfer the tortillas to a paper towel-lined plate to soak up excess oil. Sprinkle with salt.
3. Heat oil and fry the 4 eggs in sections.
4. In the same pan, heat 2 tbsp of oil. Add the salsa and cook for several minutes. Stir in sprigs of epazote.
5. Add the cooked tortilla quarters to the salsa. Flip the tortilla until well coated and cook for a few minutes. Remove from heat.
6. Serve chilaquiles with fried eggs and beans or nopalitos. Garnish with cheese, cream, cilantro, onion and avocado.

Pozole

Fantastic and flavorful pozole recipe of Mexico! The pork meat will turn tender, soft, and buttery, the aromas will deepen. Color will become as rich as the soup tastes.

INGREDIENTS

- 3 lb pork shoulder, 2-inch pieces
- Kosher salt
- Freshly ground black pepper
- 1 large yellow onion, quartered
- 3 cloves garlic, sliced
- 1 tsp whole cloves
- 1 tsp cumin seeds
- 1 bay leaf
- 4 cups low-salt chicken broth
- 2 dried chiles de arbol
- 2 dried ancho chiles
- 2 dried guajillo chiles
- 3 (15-oz) cans hominy, drained and rinsed
- Thinly sliced radishes, serving
- Thinly sliced green cabbage, serving
- Freshly chopped cilantro, serving

 Serving: 6   **Time: 4 hours**

INSTRUCTIONS

1. Place the pork in a large bowl and season with salt and pepper.
2. In a pot over medium heat, combine the pork, onion, garlic, cloves, cumin seeds, bay leaf, and broth and cover with water by 2 inches.
3. Bring the mixture to boil, cover and simmer for 1½ hours, skimming foam off top as necessary.
4. Meanwhile, in a bowl, add dried chiles and 2 cups of boiling water. Allow soaking for 30 minutes. Then blend in a blender until smooth, add more water as necessary.
5. Add chiles mixture and hominy to pot with the pork.
6. Cover and continue to simmer for 1½ hours or until pork is very tender.
7. Serve pozole with radishes, cabbage, and cilantro.

Tacos Al Pastor

Tacos Al Pastor is a favorite recipe for the people of Mexico. You can serve it with salad and tortillas. Traditional pork shoulder recipe that is easier to make.

 Serving: 10   **Time: 3 hr 15 minutes**

INGREDIENTS

- 5 lb boneless pork shoulder, ¼-inch sliced
- 3 tbsp achiote paste
- 2 tbsp guajillo chili powder
- 1 tbsp garlic powder
- 1 tbsp dried oregano
- 1 tbsp cumin
- 1 tbsp salt
- 1 tbsp pepper
- ¾ cup white vinegar
- 1 cup pineapple juice
- 1 pineapple, peeled and sliced
- For serving:
- 10 small corn tortillas
- 1 white onion, finely chopped
- 1 cup fresh cilantro, finely chopped
- 1 cup salsa
- 1 avocado, diced
- 2 limes; cut into wedges

INSTRUCTIONS

1. Mix the achiote paste, chili powder, garlic powder, oregano, cumin, salt, pepper, vinegar, and pineapple juice in a bowl until smooth.
2. In a dish, place the pork and pour the paste mixture on it. Toss to coat and cover the dish with wrap. Then refrigerate for 2 hours.
3. Preheat the oven to 350°F. Line a baking sheet with parchment paper.
4. Add 2 slices of the pineapple on the baking sheet. Take a wooden skewer and push it directly in center of the pineapple.
5. Push the slices of pork through the skewer and make a 1-inch thick layer. Push another pineapple slice on top.
6. Bake for about 1½ hours. Then allow cooling for about 10 minutes and carve off thin slices of pork and roasted pineapple.
7. Place some pork on the tortillas, followed by a few pieces of pineapple, a sprinkling of onion, a pinch of cilantro, a spoonful of salsa, and some diced avocado. Serve with lime wedges.

Sancocho

Grilled corns are perfect when served as a side for meat-eaters and vegetarians alike. Serve alongside other Mexican dishes for the ultimate feast.

INGREDIENTS

- 2 tbsp of vegetable oil
- 2 Chicken legs, pieces
- 2 chicken thighs, pieces
- 2 smoked pork chops, pieces
- 2 pork chops, pieces
- ½ lb squash, pieces
- 2 yellow onions, chopped
- 2 green peppers, chopped
- 4 cloves of garlic, crushed
- 3 green plantain, pieces
- 1 lb manioc, pieces
- ½ lb potatoes, diced
- 1 lb Yautia
- 2 cobs of corn cut into pieces
- 1 pack of coriander
- ½ pack of culantro
- 2 chorizo sausages pieces
- Salt, oregano, sour orange juice, to taste

⏱ Serving: 10   👤 Time: 2 hours

INSTRUCTIONS

1. Heat the vegetable oil in a large pot. Add chicken and pork chops, and cook for 5 minutes, until getting a little color.
2. Add a little water, smoked pork chopped and chorizo. Cook for 15 minutes.
3. In a pot, combine the squash, onion, green pepper, salt, pepper, and half of the cilantro. Covered with water and bring to boil. Simmer until squash comes apart. Let it cool and blend the mixture until smooth and creamy.
4. Fill a large pot halfway. Add cooked meat, vegetables and squash mixture. Bring to boil and simmer for 30-40 minutes.
5. Serve with white rice.

Mangu

Creamy, rich and delicious mangu is one of favorite recipes in Dominican, usually serve as breakfast! This is super simple to cook, but is full of flavor.

 Serving: 4   **Time: 30 minutes**

INGREDIENTS

Mangu:
- 3 green plantains, peeled, cut each into 4 pieces lengthwise
- ¾ tsp salt
- ½ cup water, at room temperature
- 2 tbsp butter, unsalted

Make the onions:
- ½ cup red onions, sliced
- 1 tbsp apple cider vinegar
- Pinch of salt

INSTRUCTIONS

1. In a pot, add the plantains and cover with water. Bring to boil and cook until tender. Stir in the salt. Drain the plantains and transfer to bowl.
2. Mash the plantains with the fork. Add the butter and water. Keep mashing and mixing until smooth.
3. Mix the onions, vinegar and salt in a bowl. Let rest for 5 minutes.
4. In a skillet, heat 1 tbsp oil. Add onions mixture and sauté for 2 minutes.
5. Garnish mangu with the onions and serve with eggs, Dominican fried salami and fried cheese.

Asopao De Pollo

This traditional Puerto Rican chicken and rice stew is filling and flavorful from Dominican. You can serve this delicious dish as a main.

 Serving: 4   **Time: 50 minutes**

INGREDIENTS

- 1 lb chicken thighs, boneless, skinless and cubed
- 1 ½ tsp Adobo seasoning
- 1 tsp dried oregano
- 1 tbsp olive oil
- ¼ cup sofrito
- 1 (8 oz) can tomato sauce, no salt
- 1 packet Sazon seasoning with annatto
- 1 tsp ground cumin
- 1 chicken bouillon cube
- 2 dried bay leaves
- 4 cups low sodium chicken broth
- ¼ cup fresh cilantro chopped
- 8 sprigs of fresh thyme
- 1 cup parboiled rice
- 2 corn cobs, cut into 2-inch pieces

INSTRUCTIONS

1. Place the chicken in a bowl. Season with adobo and dried oregano.
2. Heat olive oil in a Dutch oven on medium. Add sofrito and chicken.
3. Stir in the tomato sauce, Sazon, cumin, bay leaves, bouillon cube, and chicken broth. Bring the mixture to a boil.
4. Stir in the cilantro, thyme and rice. Cover the pot with lid and simmer for 25-30 minutes, or until rice is tender.
5. Add the corn and cook for 5 minutes.
6. Serve the asopao nice and hot!

Pescado Con Coco

Pescado en Coco is a Dominican recipe contain on fresh fish and sweet coconut milk. This recipe is easy and quick to cook in just 30 minutes. Fish is poached in a creamy coconut sauce!

 Serving: 4   Time: 30 minutes

INGREDIENTS

- 4 fillets grouper fish (2 lb)
- 1 tbsp lime juice, freshly squeezed
- 1½ tsp dried oregano
- 13½ oz canned coconut milk, unsweetened
- ½ cup cubanelle pepper, sliced
- ½ cup sliced red onion
- 1 tsp minced garlic
- ½ cup tomato sauce
- ½ tsp powdered annatto
- Salt and pepper, to taste
- 1-2 tbsp cilantro, chopped

INSTRUCTIONS

1. Place the fish on the plate. Season with lime juice, ½ tsp oregano, salt and pepper.
2. In a large skillet, heat the coconut milk, onion, peppers, garlic and tomato sauce over medium heat.
3. Add 1 tsp of oregano, annatto, salt and pepper. Bring to a boil and simmer over low heat for 10 minutes or until coconut milk thickens, stirring occasionally.
4. Place the fish to the skillet in a single layer and continue to simmer for 10 minutes or until cooked through. Adjust salt and pepper. Remove from heat.
5. Sprinkle with cilantro and serve warm with white rice.

Bollitos de Yuca Con Queso

This recipe is also known as cheese-stuffed fried yuca balls. These balls are crispy outside, soft and cheesy inside. A delicious recipe for your guests!

 Serving: 6   **Time: 5 hr 30 minutes**

INGREDIENTS

- 1 lb yucca, cassava, peeled
- 2 tbsp butter, salted
- 1 tsp curly parsley, chopped
- ¼ cup milk
- 1½ tsp salt, to taste
- ½ lb of cheddar, cubed
- 1 medium-sized egg
- ¼ cup all-purpose flour
- 4 cups oil for frying

INSTRUCTIONS

1. In a pan, boil the cassava until tender. Add 1 tbsp salt to the water.
2. Remove the water and puree. Stir in the butter, parsley and milk. Season with salt and allow to cool.
3. Add 2 spoonful of the mixture in the palm of your hand. Flat it and top with cheese cube. and roll around it into a ball. Repeat with the remaining mixture.
4. Whisk the egg in a bowl. Add flour in another bowl.
5. Dip the prepared balls into the egg and then into the flour to coat. Shake off the excess.
6. Refrigerate for 2-4 hours.
7. In a pan, heat the oil over medium heat. Add prepared balls and fry until golden brown. Place on a paper towel to drain oil.
8. Serve immediately.

Printed in Great Britain
by Amazon

APERTURE MASTERS OF PHOTOGRAPHY

APERTURE MASTERS OF PHOTOGRAPHY

BARBARA MORGAN

KÖNEMANN

Frontispiece/Frontispiz/Frontispice: *Cadenza,* 1940 [light drawing]

This 1999 edition is a coproduction from
Könemann Verlags GmbH, Bonner Str. 126, D-50968 Köln
and Aperture Foundation, Inc.

Subscribe to *Aperture*, the Quarterly, for just $50 U.S. for one year
or $86 U.S. for two years and you'll also receive a FREE copy of
Edward Weston: The Flame of Recognition with your paid subscription.
Write or email now to reserve your free book, a $27.50 value.
APERTURE 20 East 23rd Street, Dept. 447 New York, NY 10010.
Email: Circulation@Aperture.org. Or fax credit card orders to (212) 475-8790.

Coordination: Sally Bald and Susanne Kassung
Assistant: Monika Dauer
German translation: Ute Hilder
French translation: Francine Rey
Typesetting: Agentur Roman, Bold & Black
Cover design: Peter Feierabend
Production director: Detlev Schaper
Printing and binding: Sing Cheong Printing Co. Ltd., Hong Kong
Printed in Hong Kong, China

ISBN 3-8290-2887-3
10 9 8 7 6 5 4 3 2 1

BARBARA MORGAN

Deba P. Patnaik

Photography is a living art in which people, places, emotions, thoughts, and acts of today's world are texturally interwoven... I want to make it clear that the foremost resource is the photographer himself. It is his authentic response to life and his urge to embody it in superb photographic form that is the active root of our esthetics.

Fotografie ist eine lebendige Kunstform, in der Menschen, Orte, Emotionen, Gedanken und Handlungen der heutigen Welt untrennbar miteinander verflochten sind... Ich möchte deutlich machen, daß die wichtigste Ressource der Fotograf selbst ist. Seine authentische Reaktion auf das Leben und sein Drang, diese in erstklassiger fotografischer Form festzuhalten, sind der aktive Ursprung unserer Ästhetik.

La photographie est un art vivant dans lequel les gens, les lieux, les émotions, l'esprit et les événements du monde d'aujourd'hui forment un tout qui s'entrelace... Il est important de rappeler que la première source d'inspiration est le photographe lui-même. C'est sa réponse sincère à la vie et son désir de l'illustrer au travers d'une superbe mise en forme photographique qui constituent la racine active de notre esthétique.

Barbara Morgan,
« Esthetics of Photography »,
The Complete Photographer

Barbara Morgan lived an incredible life of friendship, social involvement, and creative activity. Her personal life and artistic pursuits were informed by similarly eclectic and inquiring esthetics and

Barbara Morgan führte ein außergewöhnliches Leben voller Freundschaften, sozialem Engagement und kreativem Schaffen. Ihr Privatleben ebenso wie ihre künstlerische Arbeit waren von einer ebenso eklektischen

Barbara Morgan vécut une vie extraordinaire, fondée sur l'amitié, l'engagement social et la créativité. Sa vie personnelle comme son œuvre sont nourries par une esthétique et une philosophie aussi éclectique que

philosophies deeply rooted in humanity and individuality. Her rooms were lined with books on subjects from archaeology and astronomy to poetry, and art. She owned volumes on philosophy, religion, and mythology from across the globe. She had read them all, marking the pages of each with questions, exclamation points, and comments. Files full of methodically organized newspaper and journal clippings filled her studio, living room, bathroom, and dining area. Letters from school children, politicians, housewives, writers, and academics packed steel cabinets.

Morgan was born Barbara Brooks Johnson in Buffalo, Kansas on July 8, 1900. She was nine months old when her family moved from the Kansas plains to the magnificent color, space, and light of a peach ranch in Southern California. From early on, her self-educated father and schoolteacher mother encouraged her intellectual and artistic

wie hinterfragenden Ästhetik und Philosophie geprägt, deren Grundlage Menschlichkeit und Individualität waren. Ihre Zimmer waren voll von Büchern zu den verschiedensten Themen, von der Archäologie und Astronomie bis hin zur Poesie und Kunst. Sie besaß Werke über Philosophie, Religion und Mythologie aus allen Teilen der Welt. Sie hatte sie alle gelesen und dabei ihre Seiten mit Fragen, Ausrufungszeichen und Kommentaren versehen. Ordner voller methodisch gesammelter Zeitungs- und Zeitschriftenartikel füllten ihr Studio, Wohnzimmer, Bad und Eßzimmer. Briefe von Schulkindern, Politikern, Hausfrauen, Schriftstellern und Professoren stapelten sich in Aktenschränken.

Morgan wurde am 8. Juli 1900 als Barbara Brooks Johnson in Buffalo, Kansas, geboren. Sie war neun Monate alt, als ihre Eltern die Prärie von Kansas verließen und in die wunderbare Farb-, Raum- und Lichtwelt einer Pfirsichfarm in Südkalifornien zogen. Von Kindesbeinen an wurde ihre intellektuelle und künstlerische Neugier von ihrem Vater, einem

curieuse, reposant sur l'humanité et l'individualité. Chez elle, les murs étaient tapissés de livres qui traitaient de sujets aussi variés que l'archéologie, l'astronomie, la poésie et l'art. Elle possédait également des ouvrages consacrés aux philosophies, religions et mythologies du monde entier. Elle les avait tous lus, inscrivant dans la marge de chaque livre des questions, des points d'exclamation ou des commentaires. L'atelier, le salon, la salle de bains et la salle à manger étaient remplis de dossiers dans lesquels elle classait soigneusement ses articles et coupures de journaux. Elle avait également des armoires pleines de lettres reçues d'écoliers, de politiciens, de femmes au foyer, d'écrivains et de professeurs.

Née Barbara Brooks Johnson à Buffalo dans le Kansas le 8 juillet 1900, Morgan avait neuf mois quand ses parents quittèrent les plaines du Kansas pour une plantation de pêches dans le sud de la Californie, là où les couleurs, l'espace et la lumière sont magnifiques. Son père, autodidacte, et sa mère, enseignante, encouragèrent

curiosity. Later in life, Morgan would recall her philosophical father explaining to her that the world was "made of dancing Atoms... and everything in it is whirling and dancing – even if it looks still." A touchstone experience for the young child, this thought would reverberate throughout her life and art.

From 1919 to 1923, Morgan attended the University of California at Los Angeles (UCLA). The program she entered was based on Arthur Wesley Dow's principles of art "synthesis." These principles hold that art history ought to be taught with equal emphasis on the primitive, Asian, and European traditions. Of particular significance to Morgan were the concepts of "rhythmic vitality" from the Chinese *Six Canons of Painting* and the Japanese notion of *esoragoto*, which means emptying the mind and becoming one with the subject of the art. "Whether my work is large or small, abstract or realistic," she wrote, "the one thing that must

Autodidakten, und ihrer Mutter, einer Lehrerin, gefördert. Morgan erinnerte sich später daran, wie ihr philosophisch geprägter Vater ihr erklärt hatte, daß die Welt »aus tanzenden Atomen besteht... und alles auf ihr sich dreht und tanzt – auch wenn es stillzustehen scheint«. Dieser Gedanke – ein Schlüsselerlebnis für das Kind – sollte sich wie ein roter Faden durch ihr Leben und ihre Kunst ziehen.

Von 1919 bis 1923 besuchte Morgan die University of California in Los Angeles (UCLA). Das Studienprogramm war nach den Prinzipien der »Synthese« der Kunst von Arthur Wesley Dow aufgebaut. Nach diesen Prinzipien sollte Kunstgeschichte zu gleichen Teilen primitive, asiatische und europäische Traditionen behandeln. Von besonderer Bedeutung waren für Morgan das Konzept der »rhythmischen Vitalität« aus den chinesischen *Six Canons of Painting* und der japanische Begriff *esoragoto,* der beinhaltet, daß man seinen Geist befreit und eins mit dem Motiv wird. »Ob meine Arbeit groß oder klein, abstrakt oder realistisch ist,«

sa curiosité intellectuelle et artistique dès son plus jeune âge. Plus tard, Morgan se souviendra des propos philosophiques de son père quand il expliquait que le monde est « fait d'atomes dansants... » et que « chaque élément qui le compose tourbillonne et danse, même lorsqu'il semble immobile ». Ce concept, véritable pierre de touche pour la jeune enfant, influencera toute sa vie et son œuvre.

De 1919 à 1923, Morgan étudia à l'Université de Californie à Los Angeles (UCLA). Elle suivit les cours d'un programme basé sur les principes de « la synthèse » de l'art d'Arthur Wesley Dow. Selon ces principes, l'histoire de l'art devait être enseignée en accordant la même importance aux traditions primitives qu'asiatiques et européennes. Morgan fut particulièrement marquée par les concepts de « vitalité rythmique » qui illustrent les *Six Canons of Painting* chinois et par la notion japonaise de l'*esoragoto,* selon laquelle il faut libérer l'esprit pour ne faire qu'un avec le sujet. « Que mon travail soit grand ou petit, abstrait ou réaliste », écrit-

be present is Rhythmic Vitality... It doesn't matter if it is dance or montage or people or nature. There always has to be the presence of energy."

It is this energy that animates her wide range of activities – painting, graphic arts, photography, book design, writing, and editing. After graduating from UCLA, Morgan joined the faculty and taught design, woodcut, and painting. During her time in California she exhibited her own paintings and woodcuts, and worked in galleries and museums devoted to both Western and Native American art. One of the exhibitions Morgan mounted at UCLA was that of Edward Weston. This was a crucial and eye-opening encounter with photography and resulted in a lifetime friendship. In 1925 she married Willard D. Morgan, the pioneer photo-historian and editor, who encouraged her to get involved in photography. She and her husband spent many summers traveling through the Southwest and studying Native American art, religion, and culture. At Willard's

schrieb sie, »eins darf nicht fehlen: rhythmische Vitalität... Es ist egal, ob es sich um Tanz, Montage, Menschen oder Natur handelt. Energie muß immer spürbar sein.«

Diese Energie belebt die gesamte Bandbreite ihres Schaffens – von Malerei, Grafik, Fotografie und Buchdesign über die Schriftstellerei bis hin zu ihrer Tätigkeit als Redakteurin. Nach ihrem Abschluß blieb sie als Dozentin an der UCLA und lehrte Design, Holzschnitt und Malerei. Während ihrer Zeit in Kalifornien stellte sie ihre eigenen Gemälde und Holzschnitte aus und arbeitete in Galerien und Museen für abendländische und indianische Kunst. Eine der Ausstellungen, die Morgan an der UCLA organisierte, präsentierte Edward Westons Werk. Diese entscheidende Begegnung, öffnete ihr die Augen für die Fotografie und war zugleich der Beginn einer lebenslangen Freundschaft. 1925 heiratete sie Willard D. Morgan, Herausgeber und Vorreiter der Fotohistoriker, der sie dazu ermutigte, sich mit Fotografie zu beschäftigen. Die beiden verbrachten zahlreiche Sommer mit Reisen

elle, « ce qui importe est que la vitalité rythmique soit présente... Qu'il s'agisse de danse, de montage, de gens ou de la nature. Il faut toujours que l'énergie soit présente ».

C'est cette énergie qui anime une grande partie de ses travaux, que ce soit dans la peinture, les arts graphiques, la photographie, l'illustration de livres, l'écriture ou l'édition. Après avoir obtenu son diplôme, Morgan devint professeur à l'UCLA et y enseigna le design, la gravure sur bois et la peinture. Durant toute cette période californienne, elle exposa ses peintures et gravures sur bois et travailla pour des galeries et des musées consacrés tant à l'art occidental qu'à l'art des Indiens d'Amérique. Morgan organisa également des expositions à l'UCLA, dont celle d'Edward Weston. Cette rencontre fut décisive pour elle car elle lui fit réellement découvrir la photographie et marqua le début d'une amitié qui allait durer toute une vie. En 1925, elle épousa Willard D. Morgan, l'éditeur et pionnier de l'histoire de la photographie, qui l'encouragea à se lancer dans la photographie. Tous deux

Martha Graham, *El Penitente* (Erick Hawkins, "El Flagellante"), 1940

behest, Barbara took photographs to accompany the articles he was writing about Leica cameras. She also assisted him by taking photographs for a series of articles on the modern architecture of Frank Lloyd Wright and Richard Neutra.

In 1930, the Morgans moved to New York and Barbara continued painting and printmaking. She had been skeptical of photography, and once told Willard, "If you just click the shutter, you are stealing reality! I can't be a thief. I must create." But soon after moving to New York, she was given the opportunity to photograph Alfred Barnes's splendid collection of African and European art. She was struck by the way changes in lighting impacted the texture and expression in the works. Other circumstances also reinforced her move towards photography. Barbara gave birth to two sons, Doug in 1932, and Lloyd in 1935, and the uninterrupted hours

durch den Südwesten der USA, um indianische Kunst, Religion und Kultur zu studieren. Auf Willards Wunsch machte Barbara die Begleitfotografien für die Artikel, die er über Leica-Kameras schrieb. Außerdem unterstützte sie ihn mit ihren Aufnahmen bei seiner Aufsatzreihe über die moderne Architektur Frank Lloyd Wrights und Richard Neutras.

1930 zogen die Morgans nach New York, und Barbara setzte ihre Tätigkeit als Malerin und Grafikerin fort. Sie stand der Fotografie skeptisch gegenüber und erklärte Willard einmal: »Wenn man einfach nur auf den Auslöser drückt, stiehlt man Realität! Ich kann nicht stehlen. Ich muß selbst etwas schaffen.« Doch kurz nach ihrem Umzug nach New York erhielt sie das Angebot, Alfred Barnes' einzigartige Sammlung afrikanischer und europäischer Kunstgegenstände zu fotografieren. Sie war beeindruckt davon, wie sich Veränderungen der Beleuchtung auf die Struktur und den Ausdruck der Werke auswirkten. Weitere Umstände trugen dazu bei, daß sie

passèrent de nombreux étés à voyager dans le Sud-Ouest des Etats-Unis et à étudier l'art, la religion et la culture des Indiens. Sur l'insistance de Willard, Barbara Morgan réalisa une série de clichés destinés à illustrer les articles qu'il écrivait sur les appareils photo Leica. Elle prit aussi une série de photographies qui devaient compléter divers articles consacrés à l'architecture moderne de Frank Lloyd Wright et de Richard Neutra.

En 1930, les Morgan s'installèrent à New York et Barbara continua à travailler la peinture et la gravure. Demeurant sceptique à propos de la photographie, elle fit une fois la remarque suivante à Willard : « Simplement appuyer sur l'obturateur, c'est comme voler la réalité ! Et moi, je ne sais pas voler. Il faut que je crée ». Toutefois, peu de temps après leur arrivée à New York, elle se vit offrir l'occasion de photographier la magnifique collection d'art africain et européen que possédait Alfred Barnes. Elle fut alors impressionnée par la manière dont les variations de lumière pouvaient modifier la texture et l'expression des œuvres. D'autres événements

Valerie Bettis, *Desperate Heart* (kick), 1944

required for painting were no longer available. However, as she put it, "Motherhood and photography *could* work."

1935 marked a turning point for Morgan's career. She set up a studio on Twenty-third Street and began experimenting with the technical and darkroom aspects of photography. It was also the year that she began to attend Martha Graham's dance performances. Barbara was instantly struck by the historical and artistic importance of the emerging American Modern Dance. Morgan's philosophical and aesthetic sensibilities, her intuitive understanding of dance as "an eloquent life force," and her experience of the sacred ritualistic Native American dances in the Southwest corresponded with the pioneering efforts of Graham and her dance troupe. Graham and Morgan immediately became soulmates, and developed a relationship

sich der Fotografie zuwandte. Barbara brachte zwei Söhne zur Welt, Douglas 1932 und Lloyd 1935, und damit war es mit der Malerei, die lange Mußestunden ohne Unterbrechungen erforderte, vorbei. Aber, wie sie es ausdrückte: »Mutterschaft und Fotografie *könnten* miteinander vereinbar sein.«

Das Jahr 1935 bedeutete einen Wendepunkt in Morgans Laufbahn. Sie eröffnete ein Studio in der 23. Straße und begann, die technischen Aspekte der Fotografie zu erforschen und in der Dunkelkammer zu experimentieren. Darüber hinaus besuchte sie in diesem Jahr erstmals Tanzvorstellungen von Martha Graham. Barbara war von der historischen und künstlerischen Tragweite des aufstrebenden amerikanischen Modern Dance überwältigt. Ihre philosophische und ästhetische Sensibilität, ihr intuitives Begreifen des Tanzes als »einer ausdrucksstarken Lebenskraft« und ihre Erfahrung mit den heiligen Ritualtänzen der Indianer im Südwesten der USA entsprachen den richtungsweisenden Leistungen Grahams und ihres Ensembles. Graham und Morgan

allaient également l'encourager à se tourner vers la photographie. Avec la naissance de Doug en 1932 et de Lloyd en 1935, les longues heures que Barbara Morgan consacrait à la peinture commencèrent à faire défaut. C'est alors qu'elle découvrit que « la maternité et la photographie *pouvaient* faire bon ménage ».

L'année 1935 marqua un tournant dans la carrière de Morgan. Elle installa un atelier sur la 23ᵉ rue et se mit à expérimenter les aspects techniques de la photographie et de la chambre noire. Ce fut également cette année-là qu'elle commença à assister aux spectacles de danse de Martha Graham. Barbara fut tout de suite frappée par l'importance historique et artistique de cette danse moderne américaine en pleine émergence. Les sensibilités philosophiques et esthétiques de Morgan, sa compréhension intuitive de la danse comme une « force de la vie éloquente » et son expérience des rites de danses sacrées des Indiens américains du Sud-Ouest correspondaient aux recherches résolument nouvelles de Graham et de sa compagnie de danse. Graham

Martha Graham, *Lamentation* (oblique), 1935

that would last some sixty years. Their correspondence attests to their mutual affection, trust, and respect. Their collaboration turned out to be historic and unique. In 1980 Graham stated:

It is rare that even an inspired photographer possesses the demonic eye which can capture the instant of dance and transform it into timeless gesture. In Barbara Morgan I found that person. In looking at these photographs today, I feel, as I felt when I first saw them, privileged to have been a part of this collaboration. For to me, Barbara Morgan through her art reveals the inner landscape that is a dancer's world.

Morgan conceived of her first book project, *Martha Graham: Sixteen Dances in Photographs* (1941) the year she met Graham; and from 1936 through the 1940s, she pho-

erkannten sofort ihre Seelenverwandtschaft, und zwischen ihnen entwickelte sich eine enge Beziehung, die gut sechzig Jahre andauerte. Ihr Briefwechsel zeigt, wieviel Zuneigung, Vertrauen und Respekt die beiden Frauen einander entgegenbrachten. Ihre Zusammenarbeit war einzigartig in der Geschichte der Fotografie. 1980 erklärte Graham:

Selbst ein hervorragender Fotograf besitzt nur selten dieses dämonische Auge, das den Moment des Tanzes einfangen und in eine zeitlose Geste umwandeln kann. In Barbara Morgan habe ich einen solchen Menschen gefunden. Noch heute, wenn ich diese Fotografien betrachte, empfinde ich es wie damals, als ich sie zum ersten Mal sah, als Privileg, daß ich bei der Arbeit mitwirken durfte. Denn für mich enthüllt Barbara Morgan durch ihre Kunst die innere Welt, die das Universum des Tänzers ist.

Die Idee für ihr erstes Buchprojekt, *Martha Graham: Sixteen Dances in Photographs* (1941), kam Morgan in dem Jahr, als sie Graham kennenlernte. Von 1936 bis in die 40er

et Morgan devinrent immédiatement des âmes sœurs et l'amitié qui se noua entre elles allait durer près de 60 ans. Leur correspondance témoigne de l'affection, de la confiance et du respect qu'elles avaient l'une pour l'autre. Cette collaboration s'avéra unique dans l'histoire de la photographie et de la danse. En 1980, Graham déclarait qu'il

« est rare de trouver, même chez un photographe inspiré, cet œil démoniaque qui permet de saisir un instant de la danse pour le transformer en un geste intemporel. J'ai rencontré une telle personne, Barbara Morgan. Aujourd'hui, quand je regarde ses clichés, je ressens ce que j'ai ressenti la première fois que je les ai découverts, le privilège d'avoir pu être associée à son travail. Car, pour moi, Barbara Morgan révèle, au travers de son art, le paysage intérieur qui est celui de l'univers du danseur. »

Morgan conçut le projet de son premier livre, *Martha Graham : Sixteen Dances in Photographs* (1941), l'année de sa rencontre avec Graham. A partir de 1936 et jusque

Martha Graham, *Deaths and Entrances*, 1945 [planned double image]

tographed more than forty established dancers and choreographers, many of whom are now considered the pioneers of modern dance. They include Valerie Bettis, Merce Cunningham, Janr Dudley, Erick Hawkins, Hanya Holm, Doris Humphrey, José Limón, Sophie Maslow, May O'Donnell, Pearl Primus, Anna Sokolow, Helen Tamaris, and Charles Weidman. Critics like Clive Barnes, John Martin, Elizabeth McCausland, and Beaumont Newhall have all noted that Morgan's work is an unmatched testament, document, and interpretation. A host of younger photographers, such as Martha Swope, Jack Mitchell, and Lois Greenfield, are indebted to her dramatic delineation of the landscape of American dance.

Jahre fotografierte sie mehr als 40 bekannte Tänzer und Choreographen, von denen heute viele als Wegbereiter des Modern Dance gelten, darunter Valerie Bettis, Merce Cunningham, Janr Dudley, Erick Hawkins, Hanya Holm, Doris Humphrey, José Limón, Sophie Maslow, May O'Donnell, Pearl Primus, Anna Sokolow, Helen Tamaris und Charles Weidman. Kritiker wie Clive Barnes, John Martin, Elizabeth McCausland und Beaumont Newhall waren sich einig, daß Morgans Werk als Zeugnis, Dokumentation und Interpretation seinesgleichen sucht. Eine ganze Reihe junger Fotografen, wie Martha Swope, Jack Mitchell und Lois Greenfield, orientieren sich an ihrer beeindruckenden Darstellung der amerikanischen Tanzlandschaft.

dans les années 40, elle photographia une quarantaine de danseurs et chorégraphes. S'ils étaient déjà établis à l'époque, la plupart d'entre eux sont aujourd'hui considérés comme des pionniers de la danse moderne. Parmi eux, il y avait Valerie Bettis, Merce Cunningham, Janr Dudley, Erick Hawkins, Hanya Holm, Doris Humphrey, José Limón, Sophie Maslow, May O'Donnell, Pearl Primus, Anna Sokolow, Helen Tamaris et Charles Weidman. Aux yeux des critiques, tels que Clive Barnes, John Martin, Elizabeth McCausland et Beaumont Newhall, le travail de Morgan est à la fois un testament, un documentaire et l'interprétation d'une époque. Un grand nombre de jeunes photographes, dont Martha Swope, Jack Mitchell et Lois Greenfield, doivent beaucoup à Morgan qui a composé cet incroyable panorama de la danse américaine.

"The moment," wrote the French poet Paul Valéry, "generates the form, and the form makes us see the moment." A remarkable feature of Morgan's dance photographs is their ability to convey the drama of

»Der Moment«, schrieb der französische Dichter Paul Valéry, »erzeugt die Form, und die Form läßt uns den Moment erkennen.« Besonders bemerkenswert an Morgans Tanzfotografien ist deren Fähigkeit, mit

« L'instant », écrivait le poète Paul Valéry, « génère la forme et la forme nous permet de voir l'instant ». Un des remarquables aspects de la photographie de danse de Morgan est cette capacité à rendre compte de

Pearl Primus, *Speak to Me of Rivers II*, 1944

mobility and immobility in an inherently static medium. Using a 4-by-5-inch Graflex, an Ikonta B, and a Model A Leica, Morgan shot the dance images not during actual performances, but in her studio, in Columbia University's McMillen Theater, and in the Henry Street Settlement Playhouse. These photographs distill and interpret the most heightened moments of action – "instants of combustion," as she called them. She spent an enormous amount of time and energy in watching performances, rehearsals, exercises, listening to the accompanying music, and in discussion with the dancers. She developed a method of previsualization that consisted of emptying the mind and allowing "memorable gestures which inspired the idea to replay." This process, coupled with her creative and technical abilities, enabled her to recreate the excitement, delicacy, and feeling of the dance in a unique fashion. Her dramatically fluid and lyrically evocative imagery portrays the essential movements of the dancers, yet never etherealizes the body into mute abstraction. On the contrary,

einem statischen Medium die Dramatik von Mobilität und Immobilität zu vermitteln. Morgan machte die Tanzfotos nicht während der laufenden Vorstellungen, sondern in ihrem Studio, im McMillen Theater der Columbia University und im Henry Street Settlement Playhouse, wobei sie eine Graflex 10×13 cm, eine Ikonta B und eine Leica Modell A verwendete. Diese Fotografien destillieren und interpretieren die Höhepunkte der Bewegung – »Augenblicke des Aufruhrs«, wie sie sie nannte. Sie brachte sehr viel Zeit und Energie dafür auf, sich Vorstellungen, Proben und Übungen anzusehen, sich die Musik anzuhören und mit den Tänzern zu sprechen. Sie entwickelte eine Methode der Prävisualisierung, die darin bestand, den Geist zu befreien, um so »prägnante Gesten [zuzulassen], die zur Nachahmung anregten«. Im Zusammenspiel mit ihren kreativen und technischen Fähigkeiten gelang es ihr dadurch, die Spannung, Eleganz und Atmosphäre des Tanzes in einzigartiger Weise darzustellen. Ihre dramatisch fließenden und lyrisch evokativen Bilder zeigen die wesent-

la qualité dramatique de la mobilité et de l'immobilité au travers d'un médium intrinséquement statique. C'est avec un Graflex de 10×13 cm, un Ikonta B ou un Leica modèle A que Morgan prenait ses clichés de danse, non pas durant les spectacles, mais dans son atelier, au McMillen Theater de la Columbia University et au Henry Street Settlement Playhouse. Ces photographies distillent et rendent compte des moments d'action les plus intenses, des «instants de combustion», comme elle les appelait. Elle consacrait énormément de temps et d'énergie à assister aux spectacles, aux répétitions, aux exercices, à écouter la musique qui les accompagnait et à discuter avec les danseurs. Elle développa une méthode de prévisualisation qui consistait à faire le vide dans son esprit pour permettre aux «gestes mémorables qui ont inspiré l'idée d'être rejoués». Ce procédé, associé à ses capacités créatives et techniques, lui permettait de recréer l'excitation, la délicatesse et le sentiment de la danse d'une façon unique. Ses images qui sont extraordinairement fluides et lyriquement évocatrices saisissent les mouve-

hands, fingers, feet, ribs, necklines, veins, and even folds in costumes are treated with sensuality and eloquence. In *Speak to Me of Rivers II*, 1944 (p. 17), for example, the interplay of space, shadow, figure, and movement crystallizes into a climactic expression of the power of the dance. Morgan expanded her ability to evoke rhythm and drama with the use of double images, executed inside the camera. *Deaths and Entrances*, 1945 (p. 15), superbly composed with regard to scale, perspective, and tonal range, illustrates the approach.

Morgan's photography has a strong social and historical sense. She chose to celebrate the human spirit – to celebrate "something human, something dedicated." Morgan saw this "something" exemplified in the dancers, who despite barely scraping by during the Depression years, gave their "energies to celebrate

wesentlichen Bewegungen der Tänzer, ohne jedoch den Körper in eine stumme Abstraktion zu entrücken. Ganz im Gegenteil: Hände, Finger, Füße, Rippen, Dekolletés, Adern und sogar die Falten in den Kostümen werden sinnlich und eloquent dargestellt. In *Speak to Me of Rivers II*, 1944 (S. 17), kristallisiert sich das Zusammenspiel von Raum, Schatten, Figur und Bewegung als einzigartiger Ausdruck der tänzerischen Kraft. Morgan erweiterte ihre Fähigkeit, Rhythmus und Dramatik darzustellen, durch Doppelbelichtungen, die in der Kamera erstellt wurden. *Deaths and Entrances*, 1945 (S. 15), eine eindrucksvolle Komposition im Hinblick auf Proportionen, Perspektive und Farbspektrum, veranschaulicht diese Vorgehensweise.

Morgans Fotografie ist von großer sozialer und geschichtlicher Bedeutung. Sie entschied sich, den menschlichen Geist zu zelebrieren – als »etwas Menschliches, etwas Hingebungsvolles«. Für Morgan stellen die Tänzer dieses »Etwas« dar, denn obwohl sie in den Jahren der Weltwirtschaftskrise kaum genug zum

ments essentiels des danseurs, sans pour autant rendre leur corps éthéré au point d'en faire une abstraction muette. Au contraire, les mains, les doigts, les pieds, les côtes, les décolletés, les veines et même les plis des costumes sont traités avec sensualité et expressivité. Dans *Speak to Me of Rivers II*, 1944 (p. 17), par exemple, l'interaction de l'espace, de l'ombre, du corps et du mouvement se cristallise en une expression intense de la force de la danse. Morgan élargit sa capacité à évoquer le rythme et le spectacle en ayant recours à l'emploi d'images doubles, prises à l'intérieur de l'appareil. *Deaths and Entrances*, 1945 (p. 15), qui est composé en termes de proportions, de perspectives et de choix de tons, est un parfait exemple de cette approche.

La photographie de Morgan a une signification sociale et historique très forte. Elle choisit de célébrer l'esprit humain, de célébrer « quelque chose d'humain, quelque chose d'engagé ». Pour Morgan, cette « chose » était illustrée par les danseurs qui, bien que survivant avec difficulté durant les années de la

Valerie Bettis, *Desperate Heart I*, 1944 [planned double image]

time, search for human integrities and solutions." The resulting images of struggle, pain, determination, and defiance are evident in photographs such as *Mexican Suite*, 1944 (p. 25), and *Lynchtown*, 1938 (p. 27).

Pushed by her quest to make photography more than just a clicking of the shutter, Morgan manipulated and experimented with images to fashion an emphatic visual signature. She described herself as a "kinetic light-sculptor." Her light drawings and photograms are an elegant fusion of lyricism, meditative spirit, and intelligence. Her light drawings, such as *Cadenza*, 1940 (frontispiece), parallel the geometry of dance and movement of contour lines and recall Francis Brugiere's light sculptures and Naum Gabo's linear constructions. Her photomontages, however, best manifest her inventiveness and daring sensibility.

Leben verdienten, opferten sie ihre »Energien, um die Zeit zu zelebrieren und nach menschlicher Integrität und Lösungen zu suchen«. So entstanden Fotografien wie *Mexican Suite*, 1944 (S. 25) und *Lynchtown*, 1938 (S. 27) – Bilder der Anstrengung, des Schmerzes, der Entschlossenheit und des Trotzes.

Angetrieben von ihrem Drang, aus der Fotografie mehr als ein Betätigen des Auslösers zu machen, experimentierte Morgan mit Bildern und manipulierte sie, um eine eindeutige visuelle Unterschrift zu schaffen. Sie beschrieb sich selbst als »kinetische Bildhauerin des Lichts«. Ihre Lichtzeichnungen und Fotogramme sind eine gelungene Fusion von Poesie, Meditation und Intelligenz. So stellen ihre Lichtzeichnungen, wie z. B. *Cadenza*, 1940 (Frontispiz), die Geometrie des Tanzes und die Bewegung der Konturen nebeneinander und erinnern an Francis Brugieres Lichtskulpturen und an Naum Gabos lineare Konstruktionen. Den besten Beweis für ihren Einfallsreichtum und ihre mutige Sensibilität liefern jedoch ihre Fotomontagen.

dépression, consacrèrent toute leur « énergie à célébrer le temps en quête d'intégrité et de remèdes humains ». Il en résulte des images exprimant des sentiments de lutte, de douleur, de détermination et de défi qui sont très présents dans les photographies intitulées *Mexican Suite*, 1944 (p. 25) et *Lynchtown*, 1938 (p. 27).

Poussée par le désir de faire de la photographie autre chose qu'un simple « clic », Morgan manipula et expérimenta les clichés pour les modeler en une signature visuelle très forte. Elle se décrivait elle-même comme une « sculptrice cinétique de la lumière ». Ses dessins de lumière et ses photogrammes sont une élégante fusion de lyrisme, de méditation et d'intelligence. Ses dessins de lumière, tels que *Cadenza*, 1940 (frontispice), épousent la géométrie de la danse et du mouvement des lignes du corps et rappellent les sculptures de lumière de Francis Brugiere et les constructions linéaires de Naum Gabo. Ses photomontages, par contre, illustrent davantage son inventivité et sa sensibilité audacieuse.

Merce Cunningham, *Totem Ancestor*, 1944

Although montage was enthusiastically practiced in Europe and Latin America in the 1930s and forties, it was alien to American photography and was widely disparaged. Even in Europe, Hannah Höch was the only notable woman to create this kind of image. Morgan's knowledge of the European avant-garde, and her friendship with Lucia and László Moholy-Nagy, furthered her interest in the genre. She was particularly stimulated by her awareness of how montage could capture the multiplicity of modern American life and the ever-increasing complexity of the contemporary world. To her, photomontages were visual metaphors – "my poems," she called them. She used a variety of techniques – superimposed negatives, combination printing, in-camera multiple images, altered scale and spatial planes, and incongruous and disparate juxtaposition – to reveal new dimensions of reality. Her work deals with themes of social concern, natural and constructed environments, and human dignity. *Hearst Over the People*, 1939 (p. 83), one of Morgan's clas-

In Europa und Lateinamerika war die Montage in den 30er und 40er Jahren eine weit verbreitete Technik. Der amerikanischen Fotografie war sie jedoch völlig fremd, und man begegnete ihr dort allgemein mit Geringschätzung. Selbst in Europa gab es nur eine bekannte Künstlerin, die diese Art von Bildern erstellte – Hannah Höch. Morgans Kenntnis der europäischen Avantgarde und ihre Freundschaft zu Lucia und László Moholy-Nagy verstärkten ihr Interesse an diesem Genre. Besonders motivierte es sie, mit der Montage die Vielschichtigkeit des modernen Lebens in Amerika und die ständig zunehmende Komplexität ihrer gegenwärtigen Welt einzufangen. Sie betrachtete Fotomontagen als visuelle Metaphern – »meine Gedichte«, wie sie sie nannte. Um neue Dimensionen der Realität zu enthüllen, verwendete sie verschiedene Techniken wie Negativüberlagerung, Kombination von Abzügen, kamerainterne Mehrfachbelichtungen, Änderung der Proportionen und räumlichen Ebenen sowie Nebeneinanderstellung inkongruenter, unvereinbarer Elemente. Ihr Werk befaßt sich mit gesellschaftlich

Dans les années 30 et 40, le montage suscita beaucoup d'enthousiasme en Europe et en Amérique latine mais ne fut pas accepté par les photographes américains qui, dans l'ensemble, dénigrèrent cette pratique. Même en Europe, il n'y avait qu'une seule femme, Hannah Höch, qui était connue pour créer ce type d'image. De par sa connaissance de l'avant-garde européenne et grâce à son amitié avec Lucia et László Moholy-Nagy, Morgan put développer son intérêt pour cette technique. Cette découverte la stimula davantage encore lorsqu'elle prit conscience de l'adéquation du montage pour saisir la multiplicité de la vie américaine moderne et l'inépuisable complexité du monde contemporain. Pour elle, les photomontages étaient des métaphores visuelles – « mes poèmes » comme elle les appelait. Elle utilisait diverses techniques – surimpression de négatifs, tirages combinés, images multiples à l'intérieur de l'appareil, échelles et surfaces planes modifiées, juxtapositions incongrues et disparates – pour révéler de nouvelles dimensions de la réalité. Son travail traite de sujets d'ordre

José Limón, *Mexican Suite* ("Peon"), 1944

sic images, demonstrates her insight and prescience with regard to the power of the corporate media today – qualities also evident in her other montages on city life and the mindless pursuit of technology, like her later piece, *Artificial Life From the Laboratory*, 1967 (p. 71). New York City fascinated and challenged her imagination. It was to her what Paris was to Balzac, a "monstrous marvel... astounding assemblage of brain and machinery in motion." For her this city of all cities represented and reflected social, philosophical, and spiritual tensions; it was a metaphor and symbol of power, greed, and alienation.

Concurrent with her social conscience runs Morgan's faith in humanity and the indomitable spirit, as exemplified in images like

relevanten Themen, mit natürlichen und künstlich geschaffenen Umgebungen und der Würde des Menschen. *Hearst Over the People*, 1939 (S. 83), eines der klassischen Bilder Morgans, beweist ihren Scharfblick und ihre Voraussicht hinsichtlich der Macht heutiger Medienkonzerne – Eigenschaften, die auch in ihren übrigen Montagen über das Stadtleben und die gedankenlose Weiterentwicklung der Technologie klar zum Ausdruck kommen, so z. B. in ihrem späteren Werk *Artificial Life From the Laboratory*, 1967 (S. 71). New York City faszinierte sie und forderte ihre Phantasie heraus. Die Stadt war für sie, was Paris für Balzac war, ein »monströses Wunder... eine erstaunliche Ansammlung von Intelligenz und Maschinerie in Bewegung«. Für sie repräsentierte und reflektierte diese Stadt der Städte soziale, philosophische und geistige Spannungen; sie war Metapher und Symbol für Macht, Habgier und Entfremdung.

Morgans soziales Bewußtsein ging einher mit ihrem Glauben an die Menschheit und den unbezwingbaren Geist, der in Bildern wie *Spring*

social, de l'environnement tant naturel que construit et de la dignité humaine. *Hearst Over the People*, 1939 (p. 83), un des grands classiques de Morgan, révèle sa compréhension et prescience relatives au pouvoir des médias aujourd'hui – des qualités qui ressortent dans ses montages consacrés à la vie urbaine et à la quête de technologie irréfléchie. *Artificial Life From the Laboratory*, 1967 (p. 71), un de ses travaux tardifs, en est un bon exemple. Elle était fascinée par New York City qui était un défi pour son imagination. Cette ville était pour elle ce que Paris avait été pour Balzac : « une merveille monstrueuse... un étonnant assemblage d'intelligence et de machinerie en mouvement ». Pour elle, New York, la ville par excellence, représentait et reflétait toutes les tensions sociales, philosophiques et spirituelles. Elle était une métaphore et un symbole de puissance, d'avidité et d'aliénation.

La conscience sociale de Morgan va de pair avec sa foi en l'humanité et l'esprit indomptable de l'homme. *Spring on Madison Square*, 1938

Charles Weidman, *Lynchtown* (Humphrey-Weidman Group), 1938

Spring on Madison Square, 1938 (p. 73), a complex and masterly montage. The spring tulip in white and the forceful dance image occupy pivotal positions in the composition and affirm the power of life and living. Photographers, Morgan held, are "visual poets" who extract "meaning and beauty... from this largely mysterious universe in which all that lives moves." In her images, even the most commonplace subject matter pulses with the vitality she so cherished – as in *Corn Leaf Rhythm*, 1945 (p. 45).

Morgan's life and art were both infused with this profound sense of energy and purposefulness. "I'm not just a 'Photographer' or a 'Painter,'" she asserted, "but a visually aware human being searching out ways to communicate the intensities of life." She possessed an innate capacity for close associations and lasting friendships with some of the most creative minds of her time, exchanging phone calls

on Madison Square, 1938 (S. 73), einer komplexen, meisterhaften Montage, seinen Ausdruck findet. Die Frühlingstulpe in Weiß und das energiegeladene Bild des Tänzers nehmen Schlüsselpositionen in der Komposition ein und unterstreichen die Kraft des Lebens und des Lebendigen. Fotografen, so Morgans Überzeugung, sind »visuelle Dichter«, die »Bedeutung und Schönheit... aus diesem weitgehend geheimnisumwobenen Universum, in dem alles Lebendige sich bewegt, herausfiltern«. In ihren Bildern ist selbst das alltäglichste Motiv von der Vitalität durchdrungen, die sie so schätzte – wie z.B. in *Corn Leaf Rhythm,* 1945 (S. 45).

Morgans Leben und Kunst waren von diesem ausgeprägten Sinn für die Energie und die tiefere Bestimmung alles Irdischen durchdrungen. »Ich bin nicht nur ›Fotografin‹ oder ›Malerin‹«, erklärte sie, »sondern ein Mensch mit visuellem Bewußtsein, der nach Wegen sucht, die Intensität des Lebens zu vermitteln.« Sie besaß die Gabe, enge Verbindungen und dauerhafte Freundschaften mit einigen der kreativsten

(p. 73) en est un exemple de par son montage complexe et totalement maîtrisé. La tulipe de printemps en blanc et l'image de danse pleine de vigueur occupent des positions pivotées dans la composition et sont l'affirmation de la puissance de la vie et de l'être humain. Pour Morgan, les photographes sont des « poètes visuels » qui extraient « le sens et la beauté... de cet univers mystérieux dans lequel tout ce qui est vivant bouge ». Dans ses clichés, même le sujet le plus banal respire cette vitalité qu'elle chérissait tant – comme dans *Corn Leaf Rhythm,* 1945 (p. 45).

La vie et l'art de Morgan sont mus par une même énergie et détermination. « Je ne suis pas simplement un ›photographe‹ ou un ›peintre‹ », affirmait-elle, « mais un être humain avec une conscience visuelle qui s'interroge sur la manière de communiquer les choses intenses de la vie ». Dotée d'un don pour nouer des liens et des amitiés durables, elle s'était liée avec quelques-unes des personnes les plus créatives de son

José Limón, *Chaconne*, 1944

and letters with, among others, Margaret Mead, Buckminster Fuller, Joseph Campbell, William Carlos Williams, Stuart Davis, and Charles Sheeler. Her numerous articles in journals, her commentaries on art and photography, and voluminous correspondence have yet to be studied in depth. A trusted friend of Berenice Abbott, Wynn Bullock, Minor White, and Ansel Adams, she was a founding member of *Aperture* magazine. "How wonderful to behold a person, who has developed all of these capacities because of her practice of living as a whole being," White wrote in introduction to a 1964 issue of *Aperture* dedicated to her work. Her original and voracious mind forged an authentic voice and style that remains with us, vivid and irrepressible, even after her death in 1992.

In *The Discovery of Meaning, and Other Essays,* Owen Barfield suggests that the camera is "an

zu schließen. So stand sie in Telefon- und Briefkontakt mit Margaret Mead, Buckminster Fuller, Joseph Campbell, William Carlos Williams, Stuart Davis, Charles Sheeler und anderen. Ihre zahlreichen Zeitschriftenartikel, ihre Kommentare zur Kunst und zur Fotografie sowie ihre umfangreiche Korrespondenz bedürfen noch der eingehenden Analyse. Sie war nicht nur Freundin und Vertraute von Berenice Abbott, Wynn Bullock, Minor White und Ansel Adams, sondern auch Mitbegründerin der Zeitschrift *Aperture.* »Wie wunderbar, eine Person zu sehen, die all ihre Fähigkeiten dadurch entwickelt hat, daß sie als ganzheitlicher Mensch lebt«, schrieb White in der Einleitung einer *Aperture*-Ausgabe von 1964, die ihrem Werk gewidmet war. Ihr origineller, aufgeschlossener Geist prägte einen unverwechselbaren Ton und einen unverkennbaren Stil, die uns in ihrer Lebendigkeit und Unbändigkeit auch nach ihrem Tod 1992 begleiten.

In *The Discovery of Meaning, and Other Essays* beschreibt Owen Barfield die Kamera als »Emblem…

époque, telles que Margaret Mead, Buckminster Fuller, Joseph Campbell, William Carlos Williams, Stuart Davis et Charles Sheeler, gardant toujours le contact, que ce soit par téléphone ou par lettres. Il sera intéressant un jour d'étudier plus attentivement ses écrits : de nombreux articles pour magazines, des commentaires sur l'art et la photographie ainsi que sa volumineuse correspondance. Amie proche de Berenice Abbott, Wynn Bullock, Minor White et Ansel Adams, elle fut un des membres fondateurs du magazine *Aperture.* « Quel bonheur que d'avoir en face de soi une femme qui est devenue ce qu'elle est parce qu'elle a su développer tous ces dons, parce qu'elle a vécu comme un être complet », écrivait White dans l'introduction du numéro d'*Aperture* de 1964 consacré au travail de Morgan. Grâce à son esprit original et curieux, elle a créé une voix et un style authentiques, vivants et irrépressibles, qui demeureront bien au-delà de sa mort, survenue en 1992.

Dans *The Discovery of Meaning, and Other Essays,* Owen Barfield voit l'appareil photo comme « un

Martha Graham, *El Penitente* (Merce Cunningham), 1940

emblem... of imagination," and the "harp of inspiration." Barbara Morgan's camera combined both dimensions; it is indeed an uncommon achievement. Her myriad ways of image-making extend the medium's possibilities. Her singular and compelling images offer an enduring sense of discovery, inspiration, and vision. They are a legacy that continues to challenge.

der Phantasie« und »Harfe der Inspiration«. Barbara Morgan führte mit ihrer Kamera beide Dimensionen zusammen – eine wahrhaft außergewöhnliche Leistung. Ihre unzähligen Methoden, Bilder zu schaffen, haben die Möglichkeiten des Mediums erweitert. Ihre einzigartigen, den Betrachter in ihren Bann ziehenden Fotografien vermitteln ein anhaltendes Gefühl der Entdeckung, Inspiration und Vision. Sie sind ein Vermächtnis, das uns weiterhin herausfordern wird.

emblème... de l'imagination » et la « harpe de l'inspiration ». L'appareil de Barbara Morgan englobait ces deux dimensions, exploit pour le moins peu banal. Ses mille et une manières de créer une image ont élargi les possibilités qu'offre ce médium. Ses clichés singuliers et irrésistibles offrent un sens durable de découverte, d'inspiration et de vision. Ils constituent un héritage qui continue à nous interroger.

Barbara Morgan's dance photographs are captioned in the following manner: the name that appears first refers to the choreographer. The following title, in italics, refers to the name of the dance. Additional information, such as the name of the dancer when available, or a particular movement within the choreography, is in parenthesis following the title of the dance.

Die Bildunterschriften zu Barbara Morgans Tanzfotografien sind folgendermaßen gegliedert: Zunächst wird der Name des Choreographen angegeben. Der darauffolgende kursiv gedruckte Titel bezieht sich auf den Namen der Choreographie. Weitere Informationen, wie z.B. der Name des Tänzers, falls verfügbar, oder einer bestimmten Bewegung innerhalb der Choreographie, werden in Klammern nach dem Titel aufgeführt.

Les légendes des photographies de danse de Barbara Morgan sont établies de la manière suivante : le nom du chorégraphe figure en premier, suivi en italique du titre du ballet. Les informations complémentaires (nom du danseur, s'il est connu, ou mouvement particulier de la chorégraphie) figurent entre parenthèses après le titre du ballet.

Doris Humphrey, *Shakers* (Humphrey-Weidman Group), 1938

Pearl Primus, *Speak to Me of Rivers I*, 1944

Martha Graham, *Extasis* (torso), 1935

Martha Graham, *American Document* (trio), 1938

Children Dancing by Lake, 1940

Girl Playing Recorder, 1945

Corn Leaf Rhythm, 1945

Pregnant, 1942

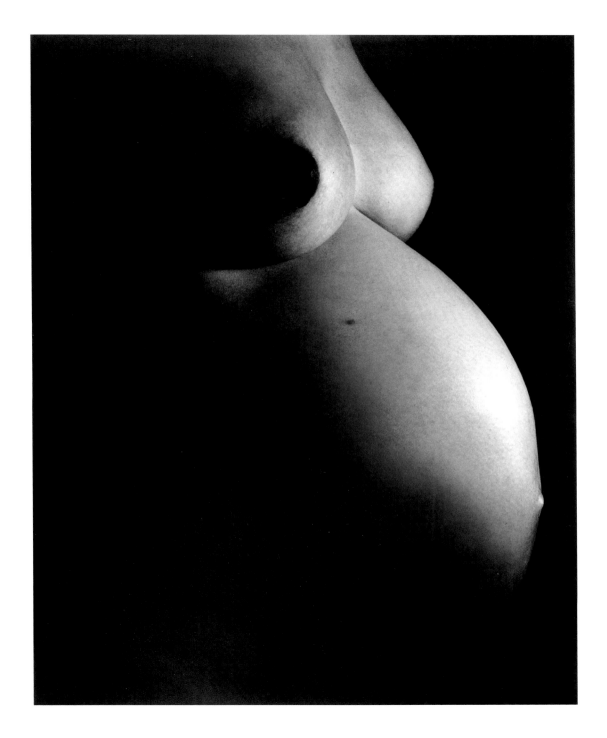

Marie, 1947

Dr. Daisetz Teitaro Suzuki, 1950

Nancy Newhall, 1942

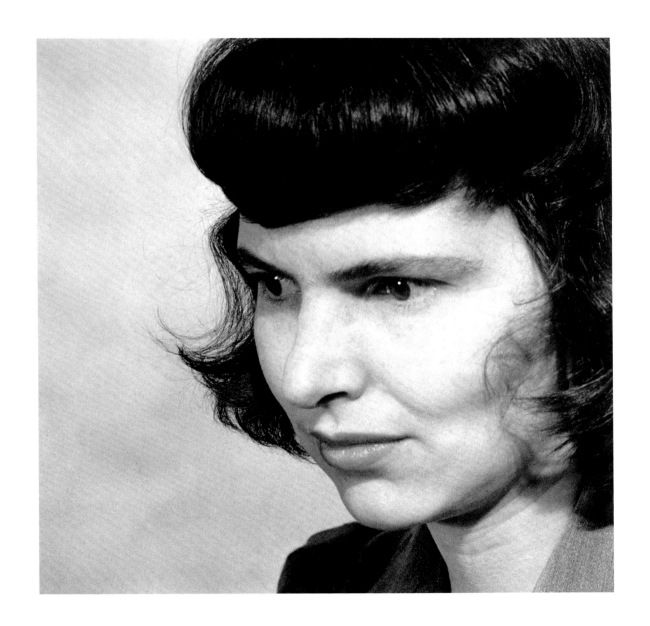

Le Corbusier in New York, 1946

New York City at Night, 1939

Macy's Window, 1939 [natural photomontage]

Kleenex, 1940 [natural photomontage]

City Street, 1937 [natural photomontage]

Fossil in Formation, 1965 [photomontage]

City Shell, 1938 [photomontage]

Fist, 1945 [photomontage]

Artificial Life from the Laboratory, 1967 [photomontage – light drawing]

Spring on Madison Square, 1938 [photomontage]

73

Briarlock, 1943 [negative-positive photomontage]

Light Waves, 1945 [photogram]

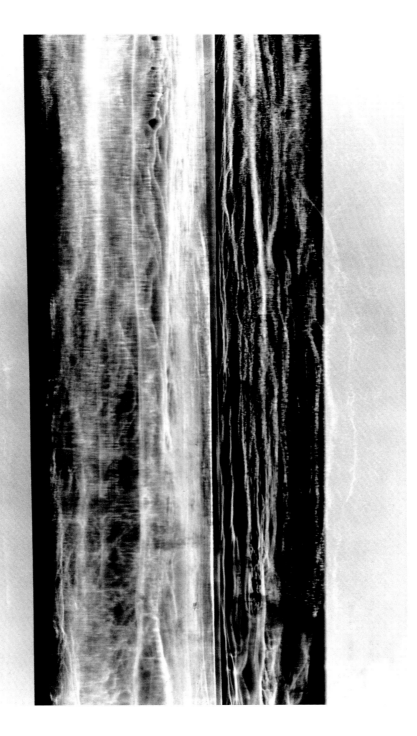

City Sound, 1972 [photomontage]

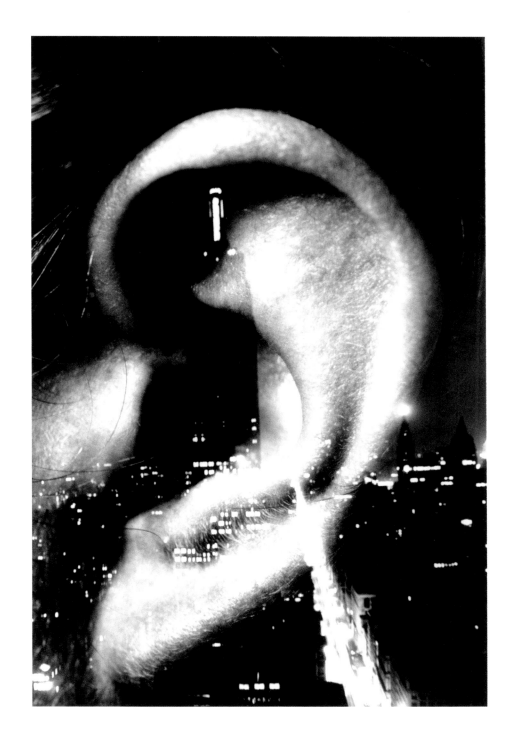

Pure Energy and Neurotic Man, 1941 [photomontage – light drawing]

Hearst over the People, 1939

Brainwashed, 1966 [photomontage]

Frolic in the Lab, 1965

Free, 1952 [photomontage]

Hullabaloo, 1959

1900 Born Barbara Brooks Johnson on July 8 in Buffalo, Kansas. Moves to Southern California with family when nine months old.

1919–23 Majors in art at University of California at Los Angeles.

1919–25 Experiments with puppetry at Gilpin Puppet Theater and lighting work at Potboiler Theater. Studies dance; hangs art exhibits at University of California at Los Angeles Art Gallery and the Southwest Museum; teaches art in San Fernando High School (1923–24).

1925 Joins Art Faculty, University of California at Los Angeles; teaches design, landscape, and woodcut. Marries Willard D. Morgan.

1922–30 Exhibits paintings and woodcuts on the West Coast. Helps Willard Morgan photograph the modern architecture of Frank Lloyd Wright and Richard Neutra.

1925–30 Meets Edward Weston and hangs his exhibits at University of California at Los Angeles. Serves as managing editor, editor, and writer for *Dark and Light Magazine* and University of California at Los Angeles Art Department. Publishes *Block Print Book* of student's woodcut work.

1930 Moves to New York City. Photographs Barnes Foundation art collection.

1931 Establishes studio in New York City; makes oil paints, lithographs and woodcuts. Exhibits at Weyhe Gallery and other galleries.

1932 Son, Douglas, is born. Continues to paint and exhibit.

1934 Solo paintings and graphics exhibition at Mellon Gallery, Philadelphia, Pennsylvania.

1935 Son, Lloyd, is born. Meets Martha Graham after witnessing *Primitive Mysteries* performance. Turns decisively

Am 8. Juli als Barbara Brooks Johnson in Buffalo, Kansas, geboren. Im Alter von 9 Monaten Umzug mit ihrer Familie nach Südkalifornien.

Kunststudium an der University of California in Los Angeles.

Experimentiert am Gilpin Puppet Theater mit Puppentheater und am Potboiler Theater mit Beleuchtung. Nimmt Tanzunterricht; organisiert Kunstausstellungen an der Art Gallery der University of California, Los Angeles, und am Southwest Museum; lehrt Kunst an der San Fernando High School (1923–24).

Wird Kunstdozentin an der University of California, Los Angeles; lehrt Design, Landschaftsmalerei und Holzschnitt.

Heirat mit Willard D. Morgan.

Stellt Gemälde und Holzschnitte an der Westküste aus. Hilft Willard Morgan, die moderne Architektur Frank Lloyd Wrights und Richard Neutras zu fotografieren.

Lernt Edward Weston kennen und stellt seine Werke an der University of California in Los Angeles aus. Arbeitet als Herausgeberin, Redakteurin und Autorin für das *Dark and Light Magazine* und an der Kunstfakultät der University of California, Los Angeles. Veröffentlicht das *Block Print Book* mit Holzschnitten von Studenten.

Zieht nach New York City. Fotografiert Kunstsammlung der Barnes Foundation.

Richtet Studio in New York City ein, arbeitet an Ölgemälden, Lithographien und Holzschnitten. Stellt in der Weyhe Gallery und anderen Galerien aus.

Geburt ihres Sohns Douglas. Setzt Malerei und Ausstellungen fort.

Einzelausstellung ihrer Gemälde und Grafiken in der Mellon Gallery, Philadelphia, Pennsylvania.

Geburt ihres Sohns Lloyd. Lernt nach dem Besuch einer Vorstellung von *Primitive Mysteries* Martha Graham kennen.

Naissance de Barbara Brooks Johnson le 8 juillet à Buffalo, Kansas. Elle a neuf mois quand sa famille déménage dans le sud de la Californie.

Etudes d'art à l'Université de Californie à Los Angeles.

Travail expérimental avec des marionnettes au Gilpin Puppet Theater et avec l'éclairage au Potboiler Theater. Entreprend des études de danse ; organise des expositions à la University of California à Los Angeles et au Southwest Museum ; enseigne l'art à San Fernando High School (1923–24).

Devient membre de la faculté d'art de l'Université de Californie à Los Angeles ; enseigne le design, le paysage et la gravure sur bois. Epouse Willard D. Morgan.

Expose des tableaux et des gravures sur bois sur la Côte Ouest. Aide Willard Morgan à photographier l'architecture moderne de Frank Lloyd Wright et de Richard Neutra.

Rencontre Edward Weston et expose les œuvres de celui-ci à la University of California à Los Angeles. Travaille comme responsable, éditrice et rédactrice de la revue *Dark and Light Magazine* et pour le département des beaux-arts de la University of California à Los Angeles. Publie le *Block Print Book* qui présente le travail de gravures sur bois des étudiants.

S'installe à New York City. Photographie la collection d'art de la Fondation Barnes.

Prend un atelier à New York City et travaille la peinture à l'huile, la lithographie et la gravure sur bois. Expose à la Galerie Weyhe et dans d'autres galeries.

Naissance de son fils Douglas. Continue à peindre et à exposer.

Exposition personnelle de peintures et d'arts graphiques à la Mellon Gallery de Philadelphie en Pennsylvanie.

Naissance de son fils Lloyd. Rencontre Martha Graham après avoir assisté au spectacle intitulé *Primitive Mysteries.*

	to photography. Begins photographing Graham.
1935–41	Photographs dancers in New York City and Bennington, Vermont, resulting in portfolio *American Modern Dance 1935–1945*.
1941	Publishes *Martha Graham: Sixteen Dances in Photographs*. Moves to Scarsdale, New York.
1941–55	Continues photographic projects and experiments. Publishes *Summer's Children: A Photographic Cycle of Life at Camp*. Designs and edits Erica Anderson and Eugene Exman's *The World of Albert Schweitzer*.
1955–59	Returns to painting briefly. Continues to photograph for brochures at Sarah Lawrence and Smith Colleges.
1959	Art and archaeology trip to Crete, Greece, Spain, Italy, France, and England.
1962	Has retrospective photographic exhibition at Arizona State University, Tempe, and University of California at Berkeley.
1967	Willard Morgan dies.
1968–88	Prepares major exhibitions in the United States and abroad. Lectures widely.
1970	Elected Fellow of the Philadelphia Museum of Art.
1975	Awarded National Endowment for the Arts Grant.
1977	Creates *Barbara Morgan Dance Portfolio*.
1978	Receives honorary Doctorate of Fine Arts from Marquette University, Wisconsin.
1988	Receives Lifetime Achievement Award by American Society of Magazine Photographers, Washington, D.C.
1991	Honored by the University of Michigan with a national seminar and exhibition at the University Art Museum.
1992	Dies August 17.

Entscheidet sich endgültig für Fotografie und beginnt, Graham zu fotografieren.

Fotografiert Tänzer in New York und Bennington, Vermont, und hält Ergebnisse im Band *American Modern Dance 1935–1945* fest.

Veröffentlicht *Martha Graham: Sixteen Dances in Photographs*. Zieht nach Scarsdale, New York.

Setzt Fotografieprojekte und -experimente fort. Veröffentlicht *Summer's Children: A Photographic Cycle of Life at Camp*. Übernimmt Design und Redaktion von *The World of Albert Schweitzer* von Erica Anderson und Eugene Exman.

Nimmt vorübergehend Malerei wieder auf. Fotografiert weiterhin für Prospekte des Sarah Lawrence College und des Smith College.

Kunst- und Archäologiereise nach Kreta, Griechenland, Spanien, Italien, Frankreich und England.

Fotografie-Retrospektive an der Arizona State University, Tempe, und an der University of California in Berkeley.

Tod Willard Morgans.

Bereitet große Ausstellungen in den Vereinigten Staaten und im Ausland vor. Hält zahlreiche Vorlesungen.

Wird zum Mitglied des Philadelphia Museum of Art gewählt.

Erhält National Endowment for the Arts Grant.

Erstellt *Barbara Morgan Dance Portfolio*.

Marquette University, Wisconsin, verleiht ihr den Titel des Ehrendoktors der Schönen Künste.

Wird von der American Society of Magazine Photographers, Washington, D.C. für ihr Lebenswerk ausgezeichnet.

Wird von der University of Michigan mit einem Seminar und einer Ausstellung im University Art Museum geehrt.

Stirbt am 17. August.

Décide de se consacrer à la photographie et commence à photographier Graham.

Photographie des danseurs de New York et Bennington (Vermont), ce qui aboutira au portfolio *American Modern Dance 1935–1945*.

Publie *Martha Graham : Sixteen Dances in Photographs*. S'installe à Scarsdale, New York.

Poursuit ses projets et expériences photographiques. Publie *Summer's Children : A Photographic Cycle of Life at Camp*. Conçoit et édite le livre d'Erica Anderson et Eugene Exman *The World of Albert Schweitzer*.

Reprend la peinture durant une brève période. Continue à photographier pour des revues publiées par le Sarah Lawrence College et le Smith College.

Entreprend un voyage culturel et archéologique en Crète, Grèce, Espagne, Italie, France et Angleterre.

Rétrospective de son œuvre photographique à Arizona State University, Tempe, et à la University of California à Berkeley.

Willard Morgan meurt.

Prépare d'importantes expositions aux Etats-Unis et à l'étranger. Donne des conférences.

Elue membre du Philadelphia Museum of Art.

Reçoit une bourse de la fondation nationale pour les arts.

Crée le *Barbara Morgan Dance Portfolio*.

Reçoit le titre de docteur honoris causa des Beaux-Arts de la Marquette University, Wisconsin.

Reçoit pour l'ensemble de son œuvre le Prix de la American Society of Magazine Photographers, Washington, D.C.

Honorée par la University of Michigan qui lui consacre un séminaire et une exposition au University Art Museum.

Meurt le 17 août.

SELECTED BIBLIOGRAPHY
AUSWAHLBIBLIOGRAPHIE
BIBLIOGRAPHIE SÉLECTIVE

BOOKS BY BARBARA MORGAN
BÜCHER VON BARBARA MORGAN
LIVRES DE BARBARA MORGAN

Barbara Morgan. Hastings-on-Hudson, New York: Morgan & Morgan, 1972.
Barbara Morgan Photomontage. Dobbs Ferry, New York: Morgan & Morgan, 1980. George Eastman House exhibition catalog.
Conquest of Civilization. New York: Harper & Row, 1938. With James Henry.
Martha Graham: Sixteen Dances in Photography. New York: Duell, Sloan & Pearce, 1941.
Prestini's Art in Wood. Lake Forest, Illinois: Pocahontas Press, 1950.
Summer's Children: A Photographic Cycle of Life at Camp. Scarsdale, New York: Morgan & Morgan, 1951.
The World of Albert Schweitzer. New York: Harper & Row, 1955. With Erica Anderson and Eugene Exman.

ARTICLES BY BARBARA MORGAN
ARTIKEL VON BARBARA MORGAN
ARTICLES DE BARBARA MORGAN

"Abstraction in Photography." *Encyclopedia of Photography*, 1963. Vol. 1.
"Barbara Morgan." *Aperture*, 1964. Vol. 11, no. 1.
"Birth and Proliferation of the Photographic Image." *Aperture*, 1962. Vol. 10, no. 2.
"Dance Photography." *US Camera*, February 1940.
"In Focus: Photography, the Youngest Art." *Magazine of Art*, November 1942. Vol. 35, no. 7.

"Is Black and White Better Than Color? No! Says Ivan Dmitri, Yes! Says Barbara Morgan." *Modern Photography*, July 1952. Vol. 86.
"Growing Americans: Shooting Stills for a Government Short." *US Camera*, February 1944. Vol. 7, no. 1.
"Kinetic Design in Photography." *Aperture*, 1953. Vol. 1, no. 4.
"Modern Dance." *Popular Photography*, June 1945.
"My Creative Experience with Photomontage." *Image*, 1971.
"The Photographer's Ego vs. An Anonymous (?) Medium." *Spectrum Magazine*, 1956. Vol. 6, no. 2.
"The Presentation Medium of Family of Man." *Aperture*, 1955. Vol. 3, no. 2.
"The Scope of Action Photography." *The Complete Photographer*, March 20, 1944.
"Under the Sun." *Aperture*, 1960. Vol. 8, no. 4. A review of the book by Lyons, Labrot and Chappell.
"What I Think of Modern Art." *L.A. Times*, June 13, 1926.

ABOUT BARBARA MORGAN
ÜBER BARBARA MORGAN
SUR BARBARA MORGAN

Barbara Morgan: Prints, Drawings, Watercolors, & Photographs. Wisconsin: Marquette University Press, 1988. Essay by William C. Agee.
Arnheim, Rudolph. "Mobility and Stillness." University of Michigan Symposium, 1991.
"Barbara Morgan: Painter Turned Photographer." *Photography*, 1938. Vol. 6, no. 7.
Bunnell, Peter. "Barbara Morgan" in *Degrees of Guidance*. New York: Cambridge University Press, 1993.
Deschin, Jacob. "Barbara Morgan: Permanence Through Preservation."

Popular Photography, August 1971. Vol. 69, no. 2.
Doty, Robert, ed. *Photography In America*. New York: Random House Press, 1975.
McCausland, Elizabeth. "Dance Photographs by Barbara Morgan." *Springfield Sunday Union and Republican*, September 7, 1941.
Neugass, Fritz. "Die vielen Gesichter der Barbara Morgan." *Foto Magazin*, July 1965.
Newhall, Beaumont. *The History of Photography 1939 To the Present Day*. New York: Museum of Modern Art, 1949. Feature on Barbara Morgan.
Patnaik, Deba. "Barbara Morgan." *Contemporary Photographers*. London: St. Martin's/Macmillan Press, 1982.

1965 *The White House Festival of the Arts*. Washington, D.C. Kodak Pavilion, World's Fair, New York.

1967 *Photography in the Fine Arts V*. Metropolitan Museum of Art, New York.

1968 *Light 7*. Massachusetts Institute of Technology, Cambridge, Massachusetts.

1969 *The Art of Photography*. National Arts Club, New York.
Spectrum 2: Barbara Morgan, Naomi Savage, and Nancy Sirkis, Witkin Gallery, New York.

1971 *Portraits of the American Stage 1771–1971*. National Portrait Gallery, Washington, D.C.

1974 *Photography in America*. Whitney Museum of American Art, New York.
La Bibliothèque Nationale, Montreal, Canada.

1975 *Women of Photography*. San Francisco Museum of Art, California. Traveling Exhibition.
International Women's Art Festival. Fashion Institute of Technology, New York.

1976 *200 Years: America On Stage*. John F. Kennedy Center for Performing Arts, Washington, D.C.
Remarkable American Women. International Center of Photography, New York. Sponsored by *Life* magazine.

1977 *The Women's Eye*. Charlottenburg Castle, West Berlin, Germany.
Women See Men. Massachusetts Institute of Technology, Cambridge, Massachusetts.

1978 *Fleeting Gestures*. International Center of Photography, New York.

1979 *America Between the World Wars*. Kunsthaus, Zurich, Switzerland.

1980 *Working Women – 1840–1945*. Whitney Museum Downtown Branch, New York.

1984 *American Dance Festival*. Duke University, Durham, North Carolina.

1987 *La Danza Moderna di Martha Graham*. Teatro Municipal, Emilia, Italy.

SELECTION OF PAINTING AND
    GRAPHIC EXHIBITIONS
AUSGEWÄHLTE GEMÄLDE- UND
    GRAFIKAUSSTELLUNGEN
SÉLECTION D'EXPOSITIONS DE PEINTURES
    ET D'ARTS GRAPHIQUES

1926 *Modern Art Workers Exhibition*. Los Angeles County Museum of Art, California.
Seventh Annual California Watercolors Society Exhibition. Los Angeles County Museum of Art, California.

1927 *Second Annual Artists of Southern California*. Fine Arts Gallery, Oakland, California.

1928 Los Angeles Public Library, California. Exhibition put on by the Los Angeles Print Group.

1934 *Contemporary American Prints*. National Gallery of Canada, Ottawa.
Barbara Morgan. Mellon Gallery, Philadelphia, Pennsylvania. Solo exhibition.

1934–35 *Motion and Response Touring Exhibition*. College Art Associate, New York.

1936 *International Olympics Fine Arts Exhibition of Sports in Art*. New York.

1958 *Art USA: 1958*. Madison Square Garden, New York.

1961 Sherman Gallery, New York. Solo exhibition.

1962 Westchester Art Society, Scarsdale, New York.

VIDEOS

"Barbara Morgan – Everything is Dancing." Video by Images Production, Cincinnati, Ohio, for Checkerboard Foundation, New York.
"Vision USA: Barbara Morgan – Photographer." US Information Agency, Craven Films, 1974.